ONE STORY, ONE MISSION, ONE GOD

Part 2: The New Testament
A Six Week Study

Cheri Cowell

One Story, One Mission, One God
Part 2

ISBN: 978-1-941733-90-5

Published by EA Books Publishing a division of
Living Parables of Central Florida, Inc. a 501c3
EABooksPublishing.com

DEDICATION

To all those who grounded me through childhood in The Greatest Story Ever Told, and to those who continued that education at Asbury Theological Seminary where God's Word is taught as a story of grace from Genesis through Revelation.

ACKNOWLEDGEMENTS

Thank you to my family who shows me every day what it means to live by faith, to my amazing staff at EA Books Publishing who show the world what it means to work with godly character, to my church family who strives to live and worship as God's Word teaches, and to all of my readers who long to know and follow God's Word—may this study bring you closer to that goal.

ONE STORY, ONE MISSION, ONE GOD
PART TWO
THE NEW TESTAMENT

TABLE OF CONTENTS

INTRODUCTION
GOD'S STORY OF REDEMPTION FROM BEGINNING TO ENDING

God's story is not two separate stories—an old one and a new one—as some believe. It is not a story of sin and punishment as seen in the Old Testament, and love and grace as seen in the New Testament. These are just some of the misconceptions *One Story, One Mission, One God* addresses by showing how God's mission has been the same from the beginning. God's story has been, and is, about love and grace from the opening scenes in Genesis and culminating in the closing act of this story at Christ's return. God's mission has been restoration from day one.

God's mission of restoration is traced in this study through touchstones in biblical history, giving a bird's eye view of the grand story. God's desire is to restore us to our rightful place and purpose, and amazingly He has invited us to join Him in His mission of restoration and redemption.

Another purpose for this study is to help readers fit all of those stories they've heard and studied into the big picture. If you are like most, you've heard the Bible taught in bite-sized pieces. But if you were asked where and how a given story works in the overarching story, you may be at a loss. *One Story, One Mission, One God* will help you tie all those stories together, and possibly view your favorites with a new lens that will deepen their meaning.

One Story, One Mission, One God is a twelve-week study with five daily lessons. It is offered in two parts as a six-week Old Testament study and a separate six-week New Testament study. Each daily personal lesson is designed to be completed in 30-minutes, and a one-hour group lesson is included for each week.

Get ready to hear God's story in a new way–as one story with one mission about the one and only True God.

WEEK ONE
THE MESSIAH—THE PROMISED ONE

Day One: Birth of Messiah

The stage is set for the most earth-shaking event in history. Although the Storyteller fell silent around 400 BC, a lot happened in the world during that time. Alexander the Great conquered most of the known world, including the Jews of Israel who were subjects of the Persian Empire. However, history tell us that Alexander had a dream that caused him to spare Jerusalem and to peacefully absorb the Land of Israel into his growing empire. The Jews were treated well until 170 BC when Antiochus Epiphanies, a Hellenistic Greek king, plundered Jerusalem, massacred thousands, burned all copies of The Law, and abolished all sacrifices. Finally, when he ordered a pig sacrificed on the altar, it sparked a revolt that led to 100 years of independent rule for the Jews. Eventually, internal strife between orthodox and Hellenistic (pro-Greek) Jews weakened them and allowed King Herod and his Roman army to take the city. This made Herod, from Edomite ancestry, their leader—a self-proclaimed king of the Jews. This is where we pick up the story again. God's story, begun in Genesis, will not be re-written by any man—self-proclaimed king or not. In a move that must have stunned heaven, God chooses to leave his heavenly throne so humankind can enter. God becomes less so humanity can become more. This was God's plan from the beginning.

➔ Read John 1:1-14.

Two genealogies present Jesus as descending from Abraham, one is through David and to his legal father, Joseph, and the other is through Jesus' mother, Mary, all the way back to the first man, Adam. Jesus' birth story is shared in two of the Gospels–Matthew and Luke.

➔ Read Matthew 1:18-21, and Luke 2:4-7.

Others testify to the identity of this newborn. Look up these scriptures and record the name/identity of the witness.

Luke 1:39-45
Luke 1:67-75
Luke 2:25-32
Luke 2:36-38
Luke 2:41-47

At the age of thirty-three, Jesus begins his earthly ministry, fulfilling a promise made to Abraham over 2000 years earlier.

➔ Read Genesis 12:1-3.

? What is the promise made to Abram that had not been fulfilled?

Having come through the lineage of Abraham, Jesus will now fulfill the promise made to Abraham. God chose a particular people to be the carrier of the seed of faith by which blessings would pour forth.

One final voice will be heard, calling God's people to repentance, before every mountain will be made low.

➔ Read Luke 3:2-6, 15-16.

? What was the baptism John offered?

_____

John baptized for the repentance of sin and he baptized with water.

➔ Read Matthew 3:13-17.

? Who, besides John, baptized Jesus and how was it confirmed?

_____

The Holy Spirit baptized Jesus, and God confirmed that baptism with the sign of a dove as well as with His voice saying Jesus was His son in whom He was pleased. The next sign of Jesus' divinity and calling was the direct confrontation from Satan in the wilderness.

➔ Read Matthew 4:1-11.

? How does Satan want Jesus to use his calling as Son of God?

_____

_____

In three ways Satan tempts Jesus to use his calling for selfish gain. Selfishness was at the heart of man and woman's first sin, and here Jesus confronts the lie of that sin head-on. Jesus rebukes these lies with Truth–God is our true provider, God is our only protector, and God is the only One worthy of our worship. Following his temptation Jesus returns to the temple where he declares publicly his mission.

➔ Read Luke 4:14-21.

? In quoting Isaiah, what are the five parts to Jesus' mission?

_____

_____

_____

_____

? What part of his mission are you more closely called to?

_____

_____

Tomorrow we will begin to look at his ministry in these five areas–proclaiming the good news, proclaiming freedom to those imprisoned, giving sight to the blind, setting the oppressed free, and proclaiming the Lord's favor.

? In what ways have you seen evidence of Jesus' mission in your own life?

_____

_____

Day Two: Ministry of Good News

Skim Isaiah 61, which Jesus quotes from in the temple, and note the Good News His ministry would proclaim.

Following His temptation in the wilderness, Jesus enters the temple and, emboldened by the Holy Spirit, makes this proclamation:

➔ Read Luke 4:16-21.

❓ What do you think He meant by "good news?"

Some have tried to limit the scope of God's Good News to just the New Testament or a salvation pitch, but if we examine what Jesus was quoting from Isaiah, then we can see that this was God's message to His people from Day One. God's Good News was and always has been salvation, redemption, and restoration all wrapped in His holiness and love. The Good News is God's story.

❓ How does this definition of Good News expand your understanding of salvation?

➔ Read Luke 4:40-44.

❓ What phrase is added to the words "good news," which Jesus describes as His purpose for being sent?

The Good News is the Kingdom of God. In a series of teachings from Luke 13 and 14, we learn more about the Kingdom of God. Look up the following scriptures and note what you learn about God's Kingdom.

➔ Read Luke 13:18-21.
➔ Read Luke 13:22-30.
➔ Read Luke 14:15-24.

The Parable of the Mustard Seed and Yeast teach us that the Kingdom of God begins small and grows. The Parable of the Narrow Door shows us that those who think they are living kingdom lives are not when they put themselves first and shun the needs of others. From the Parable of the Great Banquet we learn that those who were first invited made excuses for not accepting the invitation, so the invitation was extended to the outcast (those not expected to be at the table).

❓ Make a list of the people you know who've received the invitation but are currently making excuses. Pray for each person by name that they accept the invitation to join you at the banquet table.

Later, Jesus is asked about the timing of this coming Kingdom. His answer gives us a more complete picture.

➔ Read Luke 17:20-21.

? What does Jesus mean by saying the kingdom is in their midst or among them?

_____

_____

Jesus already announced that the Kingdom began its initiation on Earth at the beginning of His ministry with His reading from Isaiah 61. But here, Jesus also talks about the Kingdom still coming, and that can be confusing. Some theologians calls this an "already and not yet theology." Meaning that the Kingdom of God is both fully here in the person of Jesus Christ, but it is not yet fully implemented on earth as it is in heaven. However, in these passages Jesus talks about when the Kingdom will be fully known.

➔ Read Luke 17:24-25, 30-35.

? What time is Jesus describing?

_____

_____

Although those listening to Jesus on that day could not have understood, Jesus is describing what we call today His Second Coming. When Jesus comes again the Kingdom of God will be fully realized. Until that day, we are to prepare as this next parable teaches.

➔ Read Luke 19:11-27.

? What did you learn about God's Kingdom? What did the first servant do right and what did the last one do wrong?

_____

_____

To prepare for God's Kingdom He has given everyone an inheritance, a gift to be used for His glory. We don't know when Jesus will return, but when He does we want to be found showing a good return on the investment He made in us.

? What has God invested in you? What have you done with His investment that will bring Him glory?

_____

_____

Day Three: Freedom for Imprisoned

In His Kingdom Manifesto, as Jesus' reading from Isaiah 61 is sometimes called, He lists five parts to His ministry. The first–sharing the good news–we covered yesterday. Today we will look at the ministry of setting prisoners free.

When we think of prisoners today we think of those incarcerated, and certainly God has a soft spot for those within the prison walls. But Jesus makes it clear that prison walls can be built of many things. Today we will look at three types of walls, which Jesus addressed.

➔ Read Genesis 2:15-17.

? Name some of the walls this woman had.

The Jews hated Samaritans and women, especially unclean women, were less than property. Jesus went out of His way to visit this Samaritan village and to be at the well at noon when she would come to draw water. He, a Jew and a man, spoke to her–one wall broken down. She also held secrets, dirty secrets, and yet he offered her living water to clean away the dirt. Secrets, dirty secrets, have a way of making us dry and brittle, but when those secrets are brought into the open, they can be washed away by living water–another wall broken down. Finally, she'd been worshipping other gods, and these idols held her in chains. She'd sought freedom in the arms of men and in the cold embrace of false religions, but when she met Jesus she knew her chains were broken and she was free–the last wall was no longer standing. She knew freedom was found in this One True God.

? In reading this story, what walls do you have that have yet to be broken? Ask God to break down those walls so you might drink freely of His living water.

Let's look at another story.

➔ Read Luke 19:1-10.

? Name some of the walls this man had.

The story of Zacchaeus most of us heard when we were children. Yet, there is a very grown-up message about the walls of imprisonment in the story. Today we might call it the rat race, the corporate ladder, or the chase for security and achievement. Regardless of what we call it, we all know its tug on our identity, our time, and our energy. Zacchaeus could be any of us today. He was on the corporate treadmill and it had him in chains. Then word spreads that Jesus in coming to town and Zacchaeus knows Jesus won't get near him–he's so far in that deep dark well, covered by debt and deadlines. But Zacchaeus is drawn to the scene. He climbs a tree without even thinking about what he's doing. Then Jesus calls to him. He's been seen. Zacchaeus must have been so afraid because he's so covered in the sins of greed and he knows he's no good. But just as he is about to fall out of that tree to his knees, Jesus shatters his walls. Jesus not only sees him, but this godly man invites himself to dinner–at his house–at this sinner's house. Zacchaeus thought he was too far removed from God to ever have a way back, but that wall was shattered.

? What walls do you share with Zacchaeus? Ask God to come into your house, breaking down that wall, which says you are too far-gone.

One more story and another wall.

➜ Read John 8:3-11.

? What are the walls this woman and the men surrounding her had?

You might say this one is obvious–she was caught in adultery. However, this story is not only about adultery. Certainly, sexual immorality builds a wall around our hearts and it is not limited to adultery. Jesus later will say that even looking at a woman with lust in your heart is sin. Fanaticizing about a relationship that is not sanctified in a marriage is sin. Listening to, watching, reading about anything that is not edifying to your mate is sinful. But as I said, that is not the only wall Jesus tears down in this encounter. The religious leaders brought this woman, who they pulled from the bed of a married man, because they thought they could corner Jesus. The first wall Jesus addresses is the wall the men were hiding behind. Religious arrogance builds walls between us and those whom we are to serve. Some believe Jesus wrote in the sand the sins of these men, revealing them as hypocrites, but let's focus on the words Jesus says.

➜ Read John 8:7.

? What did Jesus say to the Pharisees?

Don't set yourself above, but instead extend grace, be loving, and don't cast stones because you live in a glass house. The wall of self-righteousness was removed and their sins exposed. The men slinked away.

? Do you suffer from this sin? Ask God's forgiveness and then ask Him to give you a heart of grace and love toward others.

There is one more wall, which this story reveals in a beautiful way. The woman's sin was revealed. She was exposed. Shame has a way of hiding us behind a self-built prison wall. Yet, when our shame is exposed to the unconditional love of God, we discover that wall was nothing but sand. Jesus asks the woman, "Who is here condemning you?" She looked around only to discover they'd all disappeared. "Then neither do I," Jesus said. The wall disappeared and I imagine she stood a little straighter and held her head high for she now knew that in Christ there is no condemnation.

? Are you carrying shame? Ask God to show you His unconditional love so you can experience the tumbling of that sand wall–and be set free.

Day Four: Freedom for Captives

The third part of Jesus' ministry is worded differently depending upon your Bible's translation. Some say, "setting the oppressed free," while others call it, "setting the captives free." When placed next to the second item in the list–setting prisoners free–the question becomes, "What is the difference?"

? Look up the word "captive" and record what you learn.

_____

One of the definitions for the word is 'held under control of another but having the appearance of independence.' Yesterday we used the image of a prison wall to help us explore the different ways in which Jesus sets prisoners free. Today we will use the image of a branding iron. American Slaves were often branded with the mark of their owner so if the slave were to run away, he or she would be identified as the property of their owner. The slave might think he could flee to freedom, but that branding would almost always secure his return.

Let's look at four stories of those who were branded and, yet, Jesus set them free.

➔ Read Mark 5:1-20.

? What brand had been placed on this man and what was the result?

Some translations label this story as that of a demon-possessed man. He had been branded by society as someone unclean. He lived in the caves outside of town, away from society, forgotten and forsaken. Jesus spoke directly to the evil spirit that held this man captive and He called that spirit to leave the man. The spirit left and the branding was removed. The captive was set free.

? What label are you wearing?

_____

We are good at placing labels on others and on ourselves. The good news is that Jesus sees the person beyond the label who is in need of love, compassion, and acceptance. If you are wearing a label, know that Jesus sees you and He is offering freedom.

➔ Read John 5:1-3, 5-9.

? What label was this man given?

_____

We know that for thirty-eight years he'd been sick. We don't know with what, but we know he was unable to move. Yet, he had gone to the pool of Bethesda to be healed. He wanted to be healed, which then begs the question, why did Jesus ask if the man wanted to be healed?

_____

? Do you know someone who has been sick for so long it has become his or her identity? Have you suffered for such a long time that you feel you are your illness, your situation, and your circumstance? You are so much more, and God sees you as separate from your label. That day at the Pool of Bethesda that man's label was removed because Jesus saw him as more, much more. He was set free and you can be, too.

➜ Read Luke 7:11-17.

? What was the label this boy and his mother were given?

Although the label of widow referred to a woman whose husband had died, because of the social context it actually meant a person living a marginal existence in extreme poverty. This widow is now burying her only son, her only hope of keeping her husband's land. She not only carried the stigmatized label of widow, but it now, through the death of her son, was clear to her she'd been abandoned by God.

? Who do you know who carries a label like a brand, which limits them and defines them?

Jesus removes these labels, these brands, one by one. First, Jesus saw her and His heart went out to her. No matter what label you have been tattooed with–divorcee', single, orphan, failure, wimp, stupid, or widow–Jesus sees you and His heart goes out to you. Jesus then brings life back to the boy who'd been labeled dead. Perhaps you've been dead to someone. Perhaps a torn relationship needs new life. Jesus brings new life to those relationships that need resuscitation. And he brings new life to those whose hearts and souls are dead to feelings, to hopes, and to dreams. When this son was returned to his mother, she had a new lease on life. Her label was removed and she was set free.

? What brand or tattoo are you wearing? Ask God to remove that brand and to give you new life.

These three stories have one thing in common–they are stories about those who were held captive by their labels, their tattoos, or their brandings. Whether self-imposed or imposed by society, these stories demonstrate that Jesus sees through them. He sees the person behind the imprint, and if He can set these men and women free, He can do the same for each of us today. When set free, your brand is no longer that thing which held you captive. Your new branding is–Child of God.

Day Five: The Year of the Lord

➜ Read Leviticus 25:9-13.

❓ In one word describe the Year of Jubilee.

A loud trumpet would proclaim liberty throughout the country on the 10th day of the 7th month (the Day of Atonement), after the lapse of 7 Sabbaths of years = 49 years. That is every fifty years was to be a time in which liberty would be proclaimed to all the inhabitants of the country. In a word, the Year of Jubilee was about freedom. It was to be a foreshadowing of the coming Year of the Lord, the fourth part of the Kingdom Manifesto. Jesus, indeed, set people free, as He continues to do today. However, Jesus never intended this to be a job only He would do.

➜ Read Luke 5:1-11.

❓ What did Jesus call Peter to do?

Jesus tells Peter that he will be a fisher of men. The first step in fulfilling a Year of Jubilee is to call people into the Kingdom. We do this in many ways.

➜ Read Mark 3:13-19.

❓ What two things did Jesus send these followers out to do?

➜ Read Matthew 9:35-38.

❓ What two additional things did Jesus do?

In Mark we learn that Jesus sent His followers out to preach and teach and to drive out demons. It is interesting to note that demons come in all shapes and sizes and many of the demons that haunt us are cloaked in guilt and shame. In the Book of Matthew, Jesus proclaimed or preached the good news and He healed the sick. He then called His followers to work in the fields with Him, healing the sick, those diseased with sin.

Then Jesus gave His followers instructions.

➔ Read Mark 6:7-11.

? What were they to do if not wanted?

The sad truth is that not everyone wants to be set free. Those of us who have received our freedom have difficulty understanding this, but this is why Jesus made it a point.

➔ Read Matthew 10:16-22.

? Summarize this warning.

Followers of Jesus, workers in the field, should not be surprised when they suffer. In fact, we will most certainly suffer when we are sharing our faith, doing good things, serving others deemed unworthy, and showing the love of Christ. Yet, we are to be as shrewd as snakes and innocent as doves. In other words, we are to go in with our eyes wide open, but also with tenderness that demonstrates God's grace and goodness.

? What does it mean to you to be as shrewd as snakes and innocent as doves?

Jesus further warns His followers about the cost of discipleship with these two teachings:

➔ Read Mark 8:34-38.

? What does it mean to take up your cross?

➔ Read Luke 14:25-33.

? What does it mean to count the cost of discipleship?

The cross was an ugly painful symbol of Roman oppression. Whatever crosses we must bear–loss, suffering, betrayal, and heartbreak–we must do so as a fellow sufferer with Christ. And we do so knowing that nothing we suffer here can compare to the glory we will gain with our Lord in eternity. The cost of discipleship might be the loss of friendships, of relationships with some family members, of prestige, of jobs, of reputation, and for some, it will cost them their lives. Jesus wants us to know that if we calculate the cost versus the reward, we will be willing to pay the cost, no matter what that cost may be.

➔ Read Matthew 18:18-20.

? What does it mean to you that Jesus will be where two or more are gathered in His name?

Today, in home churches in hostile nations, Christianity is spreading like a wild fire. To keep suspicion down these men and women gather in groups of two and three. When we neglect the gathering together of believers, we neglect the place of empowerment by the Holy Spirit, because the Scriptures are clear: Jesus is where even as few as two or three of His followers come together.

➔ Read Luke 10:1-11.

? What are they to tell people about the Kingdom of God?

We have come full circle. Followers of Jesus are to bring the Kingdom of God closer to earth by loving as He loved, healing as He healed, serving as He served, and teaching as He taught. When we do these things we can honestly say the Kingdom of God, the Year of Jubilee when all are set free, is nearer today because we've worked the fields as we've been called to do by our Lord.

? What are you doing to bring the Kingdom of God, the Year of Jubilee, to those whom you meet? What more can you do this week?

Small Group Study Outline

Week One Review

Prayer

Review

Begin by reviewing the daily lessons, asking for each person's questions and the insights they gained. Ask them to summarize each day's main point.

Discussion Questions

1. Reviewing the history outlined on Day One, where do you see God's hand in the 400 "years of silence?"

2. The author points to the five-fold ministry of Jesus as outlined in Luke 4:14-21 as the mission of God set forth from the beginning of time–now fulfilled in the life of Jesus. Do you agree or disagree with this premise?

3. The author says that God's Good News was and always has been salvation, redemption, and restoration all wrapped in His holiness and love. How does this change the way you see the term Good News?

4. How does the look at prison walls in the lives of those Jesus encountered change the way you view your own walls or the walls others are trapped behind?

5. How did the look at branding or labels change the way you see the ministry of setting captives free?

6. How does counting the cost of discipleship relate to your understanding of the Year of Jubilee?

WEEK TWO
THY KINGDOM COME: MINISTRY AND MIRACLES

Day One: Nature

When Jesus taught us to pray, He said that we are to use His own prayer as a model.

➜ Read Luke 11:1-4.

❓ After praising God's name, what are we to pray for?

_____

❓ What does it mean to pray for God's Kingdom to come?

_____

Some might say God's Kingdom is only spiritual, but the Scriptures paint a very different picture. God's Kingdom is universal and covers every aspect of life. It is both of the natural and physical worlds, and it is spiritual with a message also for the life we live in the here and now. Finally, it is both of this dominion and of the next. Today, we will begin by looking at how God's Kingdom addresses the natural world.

➜ Read John 2:1-11.

❓ How does this miracle demonstrate dominion over nature?

_____

When Jesus turned water into wine in His first miracle, He demonstrated that the Divine had indeed come to earth. 'Thy Kingdom' came to a wedding feast to save the groom from embarrassment. Jesus' ability to change water into wine for the benefit of a seemingly insignificant purpose sent a clear message. God will muster all things, even nature, to meet the needs of His people, regardless of how small or insignificant that need might seem to others.

❓ If you truly believed God ruled over all things in nature, what would you ask of Him today?

_____

➜ Read Matthew 8:23-27.

❓ How does this miracle demonstrate dominion over nature?

_____

When the men awoke Jesus, they were afraid. A huge storm had overtaken them and they were in danger of drowning. On the other hand, Jesus was not afraid. He knew the storm was coming, but instead of being afraid He'd fallen asleep. When we know that the One who holds all nature in balance is in our boat, we can fall asleep in the mist of life's storms.

? If you are in the midst of a storm, how do you demonstrate your trust in the One who calms the storms?

Sleep is usually the first thing to go when we are stressed. Sleep, or the lack thereof, is big business today. As this story demonstrates, Christians should be immune to this disorder, for we know who lies at the bottom of our boat. Sometimes sleep is elusive because of physical issues, but often it is directly related to stress. If you are struggling to sleep well at night, try spending the moments after your head hits the pillow praising God for His ability to calm storms. Praise Him for how He has calmed other storms in your life, and ask Him to calm the storm in your heart and mind. Then fall asleep with praise on your lips and peace in your soul.

➔ Read John 6:15-21.

? How does this miracle demonstrate dominion over nature?

John records this first time that Jesus walks on water (Matthew records the other in chapter 14, verses 22-33). In this story the waters are rough and choppy. When the disciples see Jesus out on the water, they are frightened. At times our lives gets a little rough and tumble. Then Jesus shows up. We aren't expecting Him in the rough and gritty of life. Perhaps we are embarrassed that He's found us in this place. But there He is. Truth is, He has dominion over even those parts of life that we think are not super spiritual, maybe even ungodly. He is there, too, and He has dominion in those places, as well.

? Do you have a rough and tumble, nitty-gritty, not so spiritual part of your life that you've sought to hide from others, maybe from God, too? Would you be surprised to find Jesus already there?

➔ Read Luke 5:4-7.

? How does this miracle demonstrate dominion over nature?

The men had worked hard all night. They'd tried every trick in the book, used every bit of brawn they had, and employed all the knowledge in their combined experience to catch fish. And they'd come up empty handed. Put simply; they were whooped.

? Have you come to the end of all of your experience, ability, strength, and knowledge only to find you have nothing to show for it? Describe that experience.

By this time Peter was beginning to catch on to what this Kingdom thing was about. He told Jesus they had tried it all, but because Peter knew that Jesus had dominion over all of nature he said, "We'll do what you say."

? How would things change in your life if you really believed God ruled over all, including the laws of nature?

_____

_____

This is not to say that every time Jesus will marshal all of nature to solve your problem, but He can. Believing that He can does not change God, but it changes us. It changes how we see our problems; it changes how we see ourselves in relation to our problems. It also changes how we relate to God. Finally, it deepens our faith. It deepens our trust. And it deepens our willingness to withstand the difficulties of life.

Thy Kingdom come...on earth as it is in heaven.

Day Two: Physical

The four gospels record about thirty-five separate miracles Jesus performed. These were not the only ones He did, but they are the specific ones the writers picked out, under the guidance of the Holy Spirit, to represent His ministry.

➔ Read John 21:25.

? How does John describe the number of miracles Jesus performed?

At the end of John's gospel he says that all the books of the world would be filled with the miracle accounts of Jesus if they were all written down. Miracles were one of the means Jesus used to demonstrate His dominion over the physical world–our physical needs.

➔ Read Matthew 4:23.

? The Good News is related to what?

Jesus cured *every* kind of disease and sickness. From simple things like sprained ankles to diseases like leprosy, and from sicknesses like fevers to mental disorders Jesus healed them all.

? What kind of sickness or disease afflicts you or those whom you love?

➔ Read Mark 2:1-5.

? What physical ailment did this man have?

We are not told why the man was paralyzed. He could have fallen and broken his back, or he could have had a disease that robbed him of his ability to walk. We don't know. But the amazing part of the story is the faith and determination of his friends. They believed that if their friend could meet Jesus, he would be healed. Their faith was so strong they overcame obstacles to get him before the Healer.

? Who do you want to place before Jesus? How strong is your faith that your loved one can be healed? What obstacles will you need to overcome to bring him or her before the Healer?

It is tempting to make this story about how God heals everyone who has enough faith, but that would be a misinterpretation. God doesn't always heal in the way we want, but He does always heal when we ask. Sometimes that healing comes in the form of death and the transition from this life into the next. Other times God heals the heart or the mind and not the body. God knows what we need and we must trust that He will give us what is best. So, let's be clear, this story is not about having enough faith so we, or our loved ones, can be healed. It is about having the depth of faith that says you know the Healer, who with a single touch or a simple word, can and will heal your loved one in the way that is best. It is about a faith that says you will overcome any obstacle to place that loved one at the feet of the One who has dominion over all things physical, mental, and emotional.

➔ Read Luke 17:11-19.

❓ What were the men in this story afflicted with?

Some translations say leprosy and others call it a skin disease. Whatever it was, it was among the most feared diseases of the time. Today's infectious diseases–AIDS, Cholera, Encephalitis, Malaria, Meningitis, Typhoid, Tuberculosis, and Yellow Fever–strike the same kind of fear. The amazing thing about this story is that the men called out to Jesus from a distance, and from a distance Jesus yelled back their instructions. It was only when they followed the instructions that they experienced healing. They weren't healed and *then* went to tell the priests. They left to go tell the priests *while* they were still covered in open, oozing sores. They believed Jesus had healed them, even when there was no evidence to prove it. Sometimes healing faith means believing before seeing.

❓ What healing are you believing God for?

Don't forget to praise God for that healing, maybe even before you can see it.

➔ Read Mark 5:24-34.

❓ What had this woman been suffering from and for how long?

Again, we don't know what kind of bleeding issue she had, but she'd suffered for a long time–twelve years. She'd suffered humiliation, financial loss, and perhaps worst of all, the loss of hope. She'd exhausted all of her resources and all of her possibilities. Then she heard about Jesus. She'd seen enough disappointment with all of the doctors she'd seen, so rather than risk disappointment again she decided to try another tactic. This time she'd just sneak behind the Healer and simply touch His robe. If He were who she hoped He was, that would be enough.

❓ Have you lost all hope of ever being healed? What if you could just touch the hem of Jesus' robe, would you risk it?

The risk must have been great. What if He wasn't who He said He was? She couldn't bear that final dash of hope. But what if He *was* who He said He was and she didn't try? What if you don't try? Her faith was rewarded. Her body and her hope were restored with one simple touch.

All of these stories of physical healing demonstrate God's power over our physical, emotional, and mental beings. God knows what we need and He will heal us in the way that is best. Our part is to have faith, to act on that faith, to take the risk, and to remember to say, "thank you," maybe even before we see evidence of the healing.

Thy Kingdom come...on earth as it is in heaven.

Day Three: Spiritual

The Jewish people at the time of Jesus were not looking for a spiritual savior; they were looking for a warrior king. They were suffering under Roman rule and they expected their king to set them free personally and politically. So when Jesus began speaking of His Kingdom being one of a spiritual dimension, they were confused.

➔ Read John 6:25-40.

❓ Put yourself in the place of the Jews. Would you have been confused?

Here Jesus claims His authority as the One who gives and sustains life. Life, in this sense, is both physical and spiritual. It was physical to the Israelites in the wilderness who needed manna to stay alive, but it is also spiritual, as Jesus was certainly not speaking of people actually eating His flesh. Therefore, manna was a sign of the real Bread of Life, Jesus, who would offer everlasting life.

❓ How does Jesus feed and provide for your thirst so you are never hungry and thirsty?

We still have people in this world who go to bed hungry, and some are Christians. So, Jesus is clearly not talking about filling this physical need. However, if you've ever been in a foreign land where Christians depend upon God for their next meal, you've been with the happiest people on earth. Regardless if their bellies are full, their spirits are overflowing. They are satisfied. You can be, too.

➔ Read Mark 6:35-44.

❓ Which kind of miracle was this–physical or spiritual?

Again, we have the physical need for food being met, while pointing toward a deeper, spiritual meaning. The situation began with a physical need. More than 5000 people were hungry and night was falling. There were no 24-hour groceries nearby. The crisis was real. Yet, the spiritual crisis all of us are in is just a real, but we don't see it as clearly. If we had hunger pangs or parched mouths when our spirits were empty or dry, we'd see ourselves the way Jesus sees us. Or maybe we do show signs of our spiritual hunger and thirst.

❓ In what ways does humanity show signs it is hungry and thirsty for God?

Some have described it as a God-shaped hole in our souls, and the psalmists have described it as a panting after the things of God. We see it in the ways we seek to fill that need with everything but God–entertainment, food, alcohol, risk, work, good deeds, drugs, sex, relationships, escape–and yet it is never enough. Only God can fill that God-shaped hole; only God can satisfy the panting of the human soul. The feeding of the 5000 met both a physical need and a spiritual need. They were satisfied in more ways than one.

➔ Read Matthew 9:1-8.

❓ Was this a physical healing or a spiritual one?

_____

Once again this is both a spiritual and a physical healing. And here, Jesus makes it clear that this miracle was to prove that He has dominion over the physical world, but also the more difficult spiritual world. Forgiveness was only the purview of the One True God, and here Jesus makes the statement–He is that God.

❓ Have you experienced the depth of forgiveness? Would you define that miracle as a greater one than a miracle of physical healing?

_____

The depth of sin colors how this question is answered. Let's look at another story of forgiveness.

➔ Read Luke 7:36-50.

❓ What does Jesus say about the depth of this woman's sin?

_____

The Pharisee did not see his own need for forgiveness, but the woman did. She knew her need and that Jesus offered her grace beyond her comprehension. This indeed is the greatest miracle, that God would be willing to forgive our ugliest of sins. Yet, even when the religious leaders believed this, they still struggled to understand the spiritual nature of God's kingdom.

➔ Read John 3:1-14.

❓ What was Nicodemus' question about the kingdom of God?

_____

Nicodemus admitted that Jesus was clearly from God because only God could do what Jesus was doing. And what does Jesus say to address Nicodemus? He muddies the water more–or does He? He tells him that to enter the Kingdom of God, we must be born again. Nicodemus is confused. How can this be? Jesus was not explaining a physical re-birth, but a spiritual one. And Jesus is saying He is Lord over that world, too.

➜ Read Mark 1:23-28.

? What do the spirits acknowledge?

_____

The evil spirits acknowledge that Jesus is the Holy One of God who reigns supreme over this world and the next.

? If even the evil spirits recognize the authority of Jesus in the spiritual world, what does that mean for us? What does it mean for you?

_____

_____

Thy Kingdom come...on earth as it is in heaven.

Day Four: Message

'Thy kingdom come' was not just a cute saying. It wasn't just part of a prayer that we are to say to make us feel super spiritual. When we pray, 'Thy kingdom come' it is a commitment to kingdom action.

➔ Read Matthew 5:43-48.

❔ What was the Kingdom action described in this passage?

Loving those who love you in return and praying for those who deserve your prayers is easy. Anyone of this world can do that. Only those who pledge allegiance to another kingdom can love those who hate and pray for those who are your sworn enemies.

➔ Read Luke 6:27-31.

❔ How does this passage expand on the concept in Matthew?

Kingdom living means not only loving those who don't return love and praying for your enemies, but it also means blessing them. Turning the other cheek doesn't imply becoming a doormat for others to abuse. Instead, Jesus combines this teaching with the admonition to give your shirt when someone takes your coat. In other words, we are to go above and beyond to bless those who curse us because in blessing them we might bring them closer to God. When we turn the other cheek, we take the steam out of their arguments against us.

❔ Which of these teachings do you have the most difficulty with–loving those who hate you, praying for your enemies, or blessing those who curse you?

Surprisingly, one of the best teachings on Kingdom living came in a story of death.

➔ Read John 11:1-7.

❔ Why did Jesus say Lazarus had died?

Lazarus, Mary, and Martha were dear friends of Jesus. So, the statement that his death was for God's glory must have been confusing. Furthering that confusion was the fact that Jesus stayed behind two additional days before leaving to go to His friends.

? Has there been a time when someone seemed certain of God's hand in a situation, but you had trouble seeing anything that appeared godly? Describe that time.

_____

_____

→ Read John 11:17-27.

? How long had Lazarus been dead when Jesus finally arrived?

_____

For four days Lazarus had been in the tomb. For four days his sisters had mourned. For four days Jesus had not come. When He finally arrived, Jesus told Martha her brother would raise. She said she knew her brother would one day rise from death because Jews believed the Messiah would one day bring resurrection to the dead. Then Jesus shared these earth-shattering words, "I am the resurrection and the life. The one who believes in me will live, even though they die; and whoever lives by believing in me will never die." Is that not amazing? Jesus then asked the question all of us must answer, "Do you believe?" She not only answered with a "Yes," but also with the declaration that she knew Jesus was the Messiah.

? What difference does it make in your life that Jesus is the resurrection and the life?

_____

To live by believing in Jesus in whom life finds its pulse, means we believe that Jesus can use science and doctors and EMTs to sustain and even bring the dead back to life, but that life really comes from Jesus. To live by believing in Jesus in whom life returns after death means knowing that death is not the end. This is kingdom living. But this story does not end with these statements of faith.

→ Read John 11:28-37.

? Why do you think the Scriptures record Jesus weeping?

_____

Jesus was fully human and fully God, and it was in His humanity that He identified with the human loss of His friend and the anguish of Mary and Martha. By weeping Jesus showed us that it is godly to weep with others. It is good to show the depth of our loss and grief through our tears. After crying Jesus stood and prayed.

→ Read John 11:38-44.

? Why do you think Jesus prayed out loud to God?

_____

Jesus tells us He prayed out loud for our benefit, so we would know it was God who raised Lazarus and not the man, Jesus. When a miracle happens, it is tempting to take credit for it, or parts of it. However, to live as Kingdom people, we must never take God's glory. He deserves all the credit.

? Have you ever considered why it was necessary for Lazarus to die and be raised from death? Was not the resurrection of Jesus enough?

_____

_____

If Jesus were the only one resurrected, it would be easy to say, "Of course, He was God's Son." But God wanted us to know that resurrection was not only for His Son, it was a promise we could hold on to. As members of God's Kingdom, we, too, will be raised from the dead, just as Lazarus was. Jesus waited four days before coming to the tomb of Lazarus so everyone would know that he was surely dead. Just as Jesus called to Lazarus from the grave, we will also be called. We love those who hate us, pray for our enemies, and bless those who curse us because we know in whose hands life rests. Life is precious in God's kingdom–this life and the next.

Thy Kingdom come...on earth as it is in heaven.

Day Five: Dominion

The last area covered by the words "Thy Kingdom Come" in our prayers is dominion over evil. We touched on this a bit when we looked at the spiritual dimension and how even the evil spirits recognized who Jesus was. Today we will look more extensively at our Lord's reign over this kingdom.

➔ Read Matthew 8:28-34.

? What did these evil spirits call Jesus and what were they afraid he'd do to them?

_____

Even the evil one acknowledges Jesus as the Son of God. These spirits feared Jesus would torture them. They knew Jesus reigned supreme over their world and He could do as He pleased with them.

This next story not only demonstrates Jesus' dominion over the spirit world, it also tells us why this teaching is important.

➔ Read Luke 11:14-16.

? Who were they accusing Jesus of being aligned with?

_____

The name Beelzebub means Lord of the House and is the title of a heathen deity to whom the Jews ascribed the sovereignty of the evil spirits. Some associate that name with Satan. In accusing Jesus of being aligned with Satan, they were denying His divinity.

➔ Read Luke 11:17-18.

? How does Jesus respond?

_____

Jesus basically says if I were in league with Satan, why would I be driving his minions out? Furthermore, if I were, then we would be destroying ourselves and that makes no sense. Jesus then extends His argument with an illustration.

➔ Read Luke 11:19-23.

? What was the point of this illustration?

_____

Strongmen were spirits of divination, so when Jesus uses this picture of a strongman He is saying He is the stronger one who takes away the armor of Satan with Truth and, therefore, He alone has the right to divide the plunder.

? Who do you think Jesus was addressing when He spoke of those who do not gather with Him and will be scattered? Who is the plunder?

As with most of His teaching, Jesus aims His arrows at the religious establishment who were plotting against Him. His point is clear–you are either working on His side or you are working against Him as the religious establishment were. If you choose to work against Him, you will suffer the consequences. The evil spirits knew this truth.

? What assurance does this give you about the power Jesus has over Satan and his minions?

At times it appears that Satan has the upper hand, but we can rest assured, Satan is making his last stand. He can wreak havoc only a little while longer, for Jesus has his number and it has been called. Next, Jesus turns His attention to His beloved and He offers this warning.

➔ Read Luke 11:24-26.

? What is Jesus saying to us, His followers?

Jesus wants us to know how the spirit world works so we can protect our houses–our souls. It is not enough to clean our spiritual houses. If, after we clean our houses, we don't fill our souls with those things that are good and godly, we will end up worse off than we were before. So what specifically are we to do to protect ourselves from the evil one? The Bible offers two instructions.

➔ Read Philippians 4:8.

? What are we to do?

This instruction tells us what we are to think and meditate on–if we think on the things that are pure and godly, we get more of that in our lives. On the other hand, we play into Satan's hands when we focus on the negative and all that is hateful.

➔ Read Ephesians 6:10-18.

? What are we to do to stand against the devil's schemes?

Here we are instructed to put on the whole armor of God. We witnessed Jesus do this again and again when He went away to pray. If Jesus put on His armor, should we not do the same? We are told why in verses twelve and thirteen.

? Why are to put on our armor *daily*? Why do *you* need to do this?

We are in a spiritual battle, whether we can see it or not. Satan is out to take us captive in mind and spirit, and the only way to fight this battle is with the weapons of truth, righteousness, peace, faith, salvation, the Word of God, and prayer. As we've learned all week, we are not to despair because Jesus reigns supreme over this world in all its dimensions. And He sits at the right hand of the Father praying for you.

➔ Read John 17:20-21.

? What does Jesus pray for when He prays for you and for me?

He prays that we are united as one in Him even as He and the Father are one. We can't fight Satan alone, but when we stand together with God, Jesus, and the Holy Spirit, we stand with God, and Satan loses every time.

Thy Kingdom come...on earth as it is in heaven.

Small Group Study Outline

Week Two Review

Begin by reviewing the daily lessons, asking for each person's questions and the insights they gained. Ask them to summarize each day's main point.

Discussion Questions

1. This week we used the Lord's Prayer as a framework for discussing what it means to pray "Thy kingdom come." What did you learn about these words this week?

2. This week's study looked at God's dominion over nature, the physical and spiritual worlds, the message, and over evil. Which area, if you truly believed God had dominion over, would change your faith the most?

3. On Day Four the author says, "When we pray, 'Thy kingdom come' it is a commitment to kingdom action." How does this understanding change how you see these words in the Lord's Prayer?

4. Day Five is a look at God's dominion over evil. What is our protection against evil and what should we do?

5. How have you witnessed God's dominion over the five areas covered in this week's study?

6. How do you personally square the concept of God's dominion/sovereignty and yet the continued presence of evil in this world?

WEEK THREE
THY WILL BE DONE: MAJOR TEACHINGS

Day One: Parables—Kingdoms of God

From the beginning Jesus' ministry was about the Kingdom of God. Therefore, when He taught us how to pray it was about that Kingdom–our part and His. Let us return to the prayer Jesus taught us to pray.

➔ Read Luke 11:1-4 (KJV).

? What follows 'Thy Kingdom come?'

Thy will be done, on earth as it is in heaven, sounds sweet. However, like 'Thy Kingdom come,' in the first part of the prayer, it is a request that requires something of us. To fully understand what we are asking when we say this in our prayers, this week we'll look at a series of Kingdom parables.

➔ Read Mark 2:21-22.

? What is Jesus saying about the Kingdom of God?

The Jews had a clear vision of who the Messiah would be and what His kingdom would look like. Jesus told them they couldn't simply put His new cloth on those old ideas, nor His new wine into those old wineskins. The two were not the same.

? Is this study challenging some of your old wineskins about who God is and what His kingdom looks like? What is challenging you the most?

➔ Read Matthew 13:1-9, 18-23.

? What do you understand about the Kingdom from this parable?

Some people will hear about God's kingdom but their roots aren't deep and they will be turned away easily. Others will hear about it, but again they will not have deep enough roots and, therefore, the worries of this life and the deceitfulness of wealth will choke the Word out. Finally, some will hear, and their roots in God's Word will grow deep enough to sustain them when the enemy tries to deceive. So it is when we pray that God's Kingdom will come, we are saying that we are committing to going deeper into God's Word, and to helping others go deeper, so that the Kingdom has a chance to grow in numbers and inside our souls.

➔ Read Matthew 13:24-30.

? What does this parable tell you about the Kingdom?

We hear this argument all the time–if Jesus ushered in His kingdom when He came, then why is there evil in this world? Jesus answered that question with this parable. He explains that weeds grow among the healthy plants because the Evil One planted them there. He doesn't remove the weeds because doing so will disrupt the growth of the good plants.

? When does your faith grow the most–when life goes well or when weeds surround you?

Thankfully, Jesus doesn't end the story there. He tells us what will eventually happen to those pesky, evil weeds. He assures us that the weeds' days are numbered.

➔ Read Matthew 13:36-43.

? What do you learn about the time of fulfillment when the Kingdom of God will fully be known?

Again we are reminded that this is an "already and not yet" kingdom. It is a kingdom that we experience a little of now, but look forward to the day when the angels will weed out of His kingdom everything that causes sin and all who do evil. Jesus closes this teaching on the Kingdom of God by sharing three little parables and wraps up with a fourth. Read these and record the image Jesus used and the message He was sharing.

➔ Read Matthew 13:44.
➔ Read Matthew 13:45-46.
➔ Read Matthew 13:47-50.

In each of these the kingdom of God is like something of true value. In the third, we are the ones of value. In the end of times, the 'valued' will be separated from the wicked and they will be thrown into the fire. Again, He assures us that evil will pay for all their misdeeds. When we pray that God's will be done on earth as it is in heaven, we are saying that we value and treasure the ways of God's kingdom, and we long for the day when evil will one day pay. We are saying we cling to God's promise that on that day the bad fish will be thrown into the fire where there will be weeping and gnashing of teeth.

➔ Read Matthew 13:51-52.

? What does Jesus tell us about the preachers and teachers of today?

We should expect our teachers and preachers to not only show us what Jesus said, but also how it fits together with the whole Word of God–the new treasures as well as old. We need to know not only that

God is love, but also that God is holy. We need to know that Jesus died for our sins, but also that this was His plan from the beginning. We need to know that God's mission from Day One was to usher in the Kingdom of God, not by fiat, but with us as His partners, one believer putting down roots at a time.

Thy Will Be Done...on earth as it is in heaven.

Day Two: Parables—Obedience

When we dare to utter the words, "Thy will be done" in our prayers, we are in essence pledging allegiance to this new kingdom. Another word for allegiance is obedience. Following Jesus' teaching on the Holy Spirit, His followers asked why Jesus planned to show Himself to them but not to the world. Read His reply.

➔ Read John 14:23.

? What does this say about obedience?

_____

We obey because we love. Our obedience should be our response to overwhelming love and grace. Said another way, obedience is the fruit of a grateful heart.

➔ Read Luke 6:43-45.

? What would a heart be full of it were producing obedience to the Scriptures?

_____

➔ Read Luke 6:46-49.

? What is the foundation Jesus is referring to in this parable?

_____

You are building that foundation with this study–the foundation is the Word of God. A heart full of God's Word, either produces obedience that stands the tests or it produces disobedience, which fails when the wind blows. Jesus also shared this parable to drive home this message.

➔ Read Matthew 25:31-46.

? What separated the sheep from the goats?

_____

Both the sheep and goats knew God's Word, but the goats never let it change their behavior. It never sunk into their hearts. This has been the message from God since Genesis. Your love and acknowledgement of who God is should affect you so deeply that it produces the desire to follow after Him, to change your ways and adopt His ways. We still won't always get it right, but because we have tender hearts we will know when we see someone hungry, thirsty, naked, afraid, lonely, and sick. And we will be moved to act.

We spoke of prayer earlier in this study in relation to our need to defend ourselves from the enemy. However, Jesus also spoke of prayer in relation to our obedience.

→ Read Luke 18:1-8.

? What was the point of this parable?

Some misunderstand this parable as being about God and likening Him to the unjust judge who needs us to beg Him. That would be a misinterpretation. We are the focus on the parable, which is about our need to be persistent in prayer–not because God needs us, but because when we come to end of our self-reliance we finally and fully rely on God. This parable is about obedience.

? How has your mind and heart changed as you've prayed over something for a very long time?

God knows we are stubborn people and it takes a long time for us to get ourselves out of the way so we can fully submit to Him. That is what obedience in prayer produces.

→ Read Luke 18:9-14.

? What is the point of this parable on prayer?

The teaching is two-fold. First, we are not to pray with puffed up words in public so all will hear us and think we are super spiritual. In fact, when we do so that is the only recognition we will receive. Instead we are to use simple words from a humble heart. Second, God wants us to know that He is looking at the heart of the person praying, not their fancy words or their status as a Christian. In fact, the most beautiful prayer might be the one without words but with a bowed heart.

Following Jesus' teaching on the Lord's Prayer in Luke, He shares this parable.

→ Read Luke 11:5-8.

? What does being audacious in prayer mean?

You and I wouldn't be bold in asking for something from someone we didn't believe could deliver, would we? On the other hand, if we truly believe God is the only one who can answer our prayer, our prayers become bold and audacious. Again, this teaching is not about a God who can't be bothered by our prayers, it is about us and how strongly we believe. If we truly believe, God has given us permission to be bold in prayer, humbly asking for what we need.

→ Read Luke 11:9-13.

? What does this tell you about God? What does this say about obedience?

Jesus rounds out this teaching on prayer by comparing Himself to a good father who gives His children not only what they ask, but also what they need. Ask and it will be given to you doesn't mean God will always give us what we ask for, anymore than a good father will give his children everything they ask for. Our God is better than a good father because He knows what we need better than we do. However, obedience requires that we seek, that we ask, and that we receive with gratitude whatever the Father gives because we trust Him, we love Him, and we obey Him. There is no other way.

Thy Will Be Done...on earth as it is in heaven.

Day Three: Parables—Love and Humility

One day when Jesus was teaching on the kingdom of God, a rabbi asked what he thought was a clever question.

➔ Read Matthew 22:36.

? How were they attempting to ensnare Jesus with this question?

It was a question disputed among the critics in the law. Some said the law of circumcision was the greatest commandment, others believed it was the law of the Sabbath, while others pointed to the law of sacrifices. If Jesus answered in any of these ways, He would have incited a riot. But Jesus was much too smart for that. Read His answer.

➔ Read Matthew 22:37-40.

? How does love summarize all that was written in the law and proclaimed by the prophets?

From the beginning, all that God desired was love. But humankind could not fathom the depth of that word. In fact, it took the entire Old Testament to show us what love was and still we did not comprehend. So, God became man in Jesus Christ and through His life and His teachings God tried once again to show us what love was. Still, as this situation described in Matthew demonstrates, we didn't get it. It is not until the story comes full circle in Christ's death and resurrection, and then is followed with the coming of the Holy Spirit, that we begin to get an inkling. Today, when we pray 'Thy will be done' it means we understand, to be best of our ability, that love has both a vertical and a horizontal component as these two parables attest.

➔ Read Luke 15:11-32.

? What brought the Prodigal son to his senses? What was the father's reaction when he saw his son coming home?

This parable is one of the few that helps us to see who we are and who God is. In this parable, God is the father who gives His son everything but watches as he (we) waste his (our) inheritance. When the son realizes that even his father's servants have food to eat, he humbles himself and comes home.

? Do you have a prodigal son or daughter or have one in your extended family?

No one can humble someone else; that can only be an inside job. The prodigal has to come to the end of himself before humility will bring him home. Perhaps the best part of the story is what happens when the father sees his son in the distance. He could have been angry. He could have not trusted his son's intentions. He could have been too wounded to respond, but that is not what he did. He had compassion on his son and he ran to meet him. What a great picture of God's love for us. What a great picture of what our love should be to our prodigals. What a great picture of what we can expect if we've been the prodigal and want to come home.

→ Read Luke 10:30-37.

? To make this parable less familiar, replace the word Samaritan with an ethnic group distrusted today and the man robbed another ethnic group.

? How does changing the names in this story make it more applicable today? What did you learn?

When Jesus told this story, He used ethnic groups that challenged the status quo. This parable challenged who was considered a neighbor and, therefore, worthy of compassion. When we say 'Thy will be done' in our prayers we are saying we will love when it is risky, we will love when its taboo, and we will love when it costs us everything.

? Who would you find it difficult to love as the Good Samaritan loved?

Loving in this way requires something that is most difficult.

→ Read Luke 14:7-11.

? What is it that this parable describes as necessary for love?

To love as we are to love requires us to be humble because only from a place of humility can we see others the way God sees them. In this parable, the guests at the wedding feast are seeking the best seats in the house because they saw themselves as important. But then they were humiliated when the person they considered lower than them was seated in their place. The lesson is clear, if we see others as special and worthy of compassion, care, and love, then we will humble ourselves and God's love will flow vertically from God through us horizontally to them.

"Lord, We Come Before Thee Now"
by William Hammond, 1719-1783

Lord, we come before Thee now,
At Thy feet we humbly bow:
Oh, do not our suit disdain!
Shall we seek Thee, Lord, in vain?

Lord, on Thee our souls depend;
In compassion now descend,
Fill our hearts with Thy rich grace,
Tune our lips to sing Thy praise.

In Thine own appointed way
Now we seek Thee, here we stay.
Lord, we know not how to go
Till a blessing Thou bestow.

Send some message from Thy Word
That may peace and joy afford;
Let Thy Spirit now impart
Full salvation to each heart.

Comfort those who weep and mourn,
Let the time of joy return;
Those that are cast down lift up,
Make them strong in faith and hope.

Grant that all may seek and find
Thee a gracious God and kind.
Heal the sick, the captive free;
Let us all rejoice in Thee.

Thy Will Be Done...on earth as it is in heaven.

Day Four: Parables—Gratitude and Forgiveness

Another pair of attributes that identifies a member of the Kingdom of God is gratitude and forgiveness. Yes, people who are not members of God's Kingdom can be grateful and offer forgiveness, but ours has a different quality. It also stems from a different place. As with His other teachings, Jesus painted pictures for us of what it means to be a person of gratitude from God's Kingdom in the form of parables.

This first parable is shared in the midst of the event we've already examined–the anointing of the feet of Jesus with oil by the sinful woman at the home of the Pharisee. When the Pharisee protested the woman's shameful act, Jesus shared this parable.

➔ Read Luke 7:41-43.

❓ Have you had a big debt forgiven or experienced this kind of grace from someone? Describe your gratitude.

The bigger the debt, the more lost, the greater the sin, the deeper the gratitude. Kingdom Gratitude, therefore, springs from the recognition of the gift of grace, and our gratitude is in direct proportion to the need of that grace. Yet, as we see with this next parable, there is also a counter to that truth.

➔ Read Matthew 20:1-16.

❓ What is the countering truth expressed in this parable?

Regardless of how deep one's gratitude, it is easy for us to take our eyes off the gift when we compare our "gift" to another's. Often our comparison comes when we measure how long we've been faithful against how long someone else has toiled in the kingdom (or not toiled). Truth is, whether someone else receives the same reward as we've received and are less deserving or more deserving, has invested more or invested less, that should not diminish our gratitude—unless we've taken our eyes off of the Giver of the gift and our own need for the gift of grace.

❓ Is there someone with whom you always come out on the short end of the stick when playing the comparison game?

❓ How would your relationship with this person change if you changed your focus from comparison toward gratitude for the gift you've received?

We always lose the comparison game. To pray 'Thy will be done' means we are grateful for the gift of grace we've received and we refuse to play the comparison game. Instead we will choose to focus on rejoicing in a God of tremendous grace–grace that is greater than all our sin.

→ Read Matthew 18:23-35.

? What is the point of this parable?

When we focus on the gift of grace and allow gratitude to fill our hearts, the change that ought to take place there is a desire to extend that grace to someone else. But as this parable shows us, that is not a natural desire. Our nature is selfish, and without much thought we easily slip back into our selfish natures. The only way we become people of grace is by holding the teaching on gratitude in the same hand with the teaching on forgiveness. This is also what makes Kingdom Gratitude different than the world's gratitude.

→ Read Matthew 6:14-15.

? If we withhold forgiveness, what will happen to our sins?

Unless we obey this command, our own sins will not be forgiven. There is no wiggle room here. Notice that Jesus doesn't say forgive those who ask for it, those who deserve to be forgiven, or when you feel like you can. Forgiveness is a command. It is a willful act. The amazing thing we experience when we obey this command is a change in our hearts. It makes it easier for us to extend grace and forgiveness to others because we know we've received what we don't deserve from a Gracious God.

→ Read Matthew 5:23-24.

? How does this teaching add to your understanding of forgiveness?

Forgiveness extends to those who might hold something against us. We may not think it rises to the level of needing forgiveness, but if there is any division between us and someone else, we cannot pretend there is nothing wrong.

? Is there someone the Lord has brought to your mind with whom you need to make amends? Determine to take steps to reconcile before the sun goes down.

Praying 'Thy will be done' means accepting the grace offered you with great gratitude, and then extending that grace to others. It means refusing to play the comparison game and instead choosing to focus on the Giver of the gift. It requires forgiving others as an act of obedience, and making amends so your worship will not be hindered. Once again, 'Thy will be done' is not a sweet phrase we say by rote in church. When we say those words it means we are agreeing to become, to the best of our ability, people with Kingdom Gratitude and Forgiveness.

Thy Will Be Done...on earth as it is in heaven.

Day Five: Parables—Judgment and Future

As we close out our look this week on the parables that help us to fully appreciate the words 'Thy will be done' in the Lord's Prayer, we need to look at the major teachings on judgment and the future. Kingdom People are future oriented, looking toward a future when final judgment will occur and Satan will fall. It also means we look to a glorious future when we will join all of the saints in our heavenly home. So who will endure the judgment and who will rejoice in glory?

➔ Read Matthew 21:33-45.

? Who are the tenants in this story?

The Chief Priests and the Pharisees killed the Son. They also rejected the cornerstone, who is Jesus. All who reject Jesus will be judged. Let's be clear, rejection is not the same as doubt. We can doubt and not reject. Rejection is often a little more complicated than what we see on the outside. Thankfully, the Lord says He judges the heart.

? Who are you praying for right now that they will come to saving faith? List the names of the people you are praying for.

Only God can see into someone's heart, and He knows when someone has outright rejected and when someone has so much baggage that he or she has a difficult time truly accepting. That fine line is only God's to judge. Nevertheless, judgment will come and we don't know when our number will be called.

➔ Read Luke 12:13-21.

? What is the risk of waiting to make that decision?

It is human nature to think we have all the time in the world. But none of us are guaranteed another day or another hour. If you've put off making your heart right with God, don't let another minute go by. And pray fervently for your family and friends who've yet to make a commitment to God because they might not have more time.

There is another kind of alertness Kingdom People are called to appreciate.

➔ Read Mark 13:33-37.

? What are we watching for?

This is watching and waiting for the Lord's return. We are to be ready, waiting and ready for Jesus to come as He promised He would. When He returns we don't won't to be found sleeping–not that we aren't supposed to sleep. That would be silly. No, we are not to be found sleeping on the job. In other words, we are to be found living Kingdom lives as fully and completely as we can. Kingdom People live in anticipation that at any moment Jesus could return and we want Him to find us faithful.

➔ Read Luke 12:35-38.

? What is the point of this parable?

Always be prepared. Let your loins be girded–hike up your robe and be ready to run–and keep your lamps burning–even in the dark hours of night. Wedding feasts could last for as long as a week, so the time of the Master's return was not always predictable. Constant vigilance is expected of every believer. Jesus also throws in a twist.

➔ Read Luke 12:39-40.

? What is meant by this comparison?

Just as we would never leave our house unprotected if we knew a robber was going to break in, so the disciple should be ready for the Lord's return. The thief image helps us to see we are at great spiritual risk when we are unprepared.

➔ Read Luke 12:41-48.

? Who does Jesus say will suffer greater judgment?

First there is the servant who exercises poor judgment and simply does not do what he knows he ought to do. This servant will suffer a beating. We don't know what this translates to but it won't be pleasant. Then there is the servant who is blatantly disobedient and who does what he knows God forbids. This servant is dismembered. Again, we don't know exactly what this means but it is horrible and a fate no believer desires. In the end the teaching is clear–from everyone who has been given much, much will be demanded; and when Jesus returns we all want to be found faithful.

➔ Read Luke 25:1-13.

? What do you think the oil in this parable represents?

This beloved parable is often taught as one about being prepared, but without understanding what the oil was, which the foolish virgins ran out of, the real point is missed. Oil is an image connected with the Holy Spirit. The Ten Virgins all started out with oil in their lamps, but the foolish ones did not prepare well and when the bridegroom did not return when they expected, they ran out.

? What causes you to run out of Holy Spirit fuel?

It is easy for us to keep our lamps filled with the oil of the Holy Spirit when life is going well. We can sing praise songs in church on Sunday and touch base with God throughout the week with a little oil left on Sunday if life is smooth. But when life throws curve balls–when the "C" word is mentioned in the doctor's office, when the demands on our time are more than the time we have, and when we just can't take another news story about how bad the world has gotten–the oil in our lamps evaporates. As this parable reminds us, we can't borrow from our brothers and sisters when the trumpet blows. Until Christ's return we need to be prepared, praying and filling our lamps with Holy Spirit fuel...

Thy Will Be Done...on earth as it is in heaven.

Small Group Study Outline

Week Three Review

Begin by reviewing the daily lessons, asking for each person's questions and the insights they gained. Ask them to summarize each day's main point.

Discussion Questions

1. This week we looked at a few parables Jesus taught and how they help us to understand what we mean when we pray "Thy will be done." Which parable helped you the most in understanding this part of the Lord's Prayer?

2. Parables exploring obedience, love, and humility were examined this week. Which parable is the most difficult for you? Did the author help you in your understanding or application of the truths in that parable?

3. On Day Three the author makes the point that God's message has been about His love but humankind could not fathom that love. Do you agree? Do we still struggle with this today? Do you?

4. If you have the ability to listen to the hymn from Day Three, do so now. Review the words–how do they illumine the message for this week?

5. On Day Four the author says that while others can offer gratitude and forgiveness, what we offer has a different quality. Can you describe the differences? How do the parables discussed this day help answer this question?

6. Is it scary to pray, "Thy will be done," in light of the last day's study on judgment?

7. The author refers to the concept of Holy Spirit fuel. Do you like this analogy? What fuels you and what drains you of Holy Spirit fuel?

WEEK FOUR
ON EARTH AS IT IS IN HEAVEN: DEATH AND RESURRECTION

Day One: Last Supper

From the opening scene in Genesis, Jesus was there. And from humanity's first act of disobedience in The Fall, Jesus was the plan. He was not a New Testament plan–He was *the* plan all along. And from Jesus' birth and through His ministry, this week had been the goal.

➜ Read Luke 22:14-16.

? It began with the sharing of what meal?

It is not a coincidence that this was the Passover meal. If you remember, the meal celebrated the shedding of the lamb's blood, which was spread over the doorposts in the Exodus allowing the angel of death to pass over that house. In this new Passover, which Jesus is instituting, Jesus is the lamb and His sacrifice will allow death to pass us over, re-writing earthly death as a passing through to a new life.

➜ Read Luke 22:19-20.

? What is the old covenant and the new one Jesus is referring to?

The old covenant was the agreement between God and His people at Mt. Sinai where they agreed to be who God asked them to be–Holy even as He was Holy. But time and again we learned through history that we were not capable of fulfilling our part of the agreement.

➜ Read Jeremiah 31:31-34.

? What did you learn about the new covenant?

This new covenant would empower us to live as God's people from the inside out. At the time, this must not have made any sense to the disciples. Jesus then did something that really confused them, especially Peter.

➜ Read John 13:2-9.

? Why did Peter protest?

Peter had acknowledged Jesus as the Messiah and in his mind the Messiah did not wash feet. But the washing of feet was a direct confrontation to the belief in a warrior king. Instead, Jesus was fulfilling the prophecy of a suffering servant king.

➔ Read Isaiah 53:1-5.

➔ Read John 13:12-17.

❓ What does it mean that we should wash the feet of others?

We are to serve as He served. We are to meet the physical needs of others and then wash their hearts clean with the blood of Jesus. Next, Jesus tells of the place He will be going.

➔ Read John 14:1-7.

❓ What does Jesus tell us about this place?

Jesus tells us there is a room in His Father's mansion for you and for me. He also tells us He will return to get us.

❓ What does it mean when Jesus tells us that we know the way to get there? What is this way?

Jesus modeled for us exactly what God meant by "Be holy because I am holy." Those early followers of Jesus became known as followers of The Way, or Christians. The Way doesn't just mean a way to get into heaven–it means a way of living life here and now. It is Kingdom living on earth as it is in heaven. However, without this next part of the plan, we would fail at this task just as assuredly as we failed through time.

➔ Read John 14:15-21.

❓ Who will empower us to live as Kingdom People?

What Jesus will do on the cross and in the tomb are paramount to changing the trajectory of God's creation, but equally so is the sending of The Advocate–the Holy Spirit, the Spirit of Truth, the Third Person of the Trinity. Without the Holy Spirit you and I are just as powerless as God's People were to live as Kingdom People throughout the Old Testament.

But it is not only the Holy Spirit that we have working on our side.

➔ Read John 15:9-17.

❓ What does Jesus call the disciples and us–what does this mean to you?

Jesus could rightly call us His servants, but instead He calls us friends. What a humbling thing to hear. The God of Creation, the Savior of the World calls you and me His friends.

? What makes for a good friend?

_____

A good friend knows what makes you happy, a friend knows your favorite meal and what makes you laugh. A true friend tells you the truth in love, and knows when to talk and when to just sit by your side. A real friend's heart breaks when your heart breaks and rejoices when you rejoice. God's love, Jesus' love, is that of a friend's. Are you a good friend to Jesus?

_____

End today by reading the prayer Jesus prayed over His disciples and over you.

➔ Read John 17.

? Make notes of what stands out for you.

_____

_____

_____

Day Two: Arrest and Trial

The unthinkable happens–and Jesus doesn't rise up against His enemies. He doesn't fight back. The disciples believed Jesus was the Messiah, but they didn't expect this. Yet, it had been predicted.

➔ Read Isaiah 53:3.

❓ What was to be the Messiah's fate?

_____

➔ Read Matthew 26:31-35.

❓ How does this fulfill the prophecy?

_____

_____

The sheep would scatter, and His friends would hide their faces from Him. This must have wounded Jesus more than the nails later placed in His hands. Betrayal breaks the heart. We see this agony play out in the garden.

➔ Read Matthew 26:36-46.

❓ What does Jesus admonish the disciples to not fall prey to?

_____

Jesus warns the disciples to stay awake and pray, lest they fall to temptation. Prayer is our only weapon against spiritual temptation, and it is clear this is a battleground. In His prayer, Jesus fights the battle to give into that age-old sin–selfishness, and He wins. "Thy will be done," He says. And God's will is swiftly enacted.

➔ Read John 18:1-12.

❓ How is Jesus betrayed?

_____

He is betrayed with a kiss. How sad. Quickly Jesus is led to the house of Annas, president of the Sanhedrin.

➔ Read John 18:12-14, 19-24.
➔ Read Isaiah 50:6.

❓ What prophecy was met at the house of Annas?

_____

Jesus was spit upon and mocked. He was slapped and yet, Jesus turned His cheek. Meanwhile, a prediction Jesus made came true.

→ Read Luke 22:54-65.

→ Read Psalm 41:9. Peter no doubt remembered this Psalm when the rooster crowed three times.

? Have you felt the guilt Peter must have felt? Describe the depth of that pain.

_____

→ Read Isaiah 53:7-8 and note in the following Scriptures where this prophecy is fulfilled.

→ Read Luke 22:66-71.

→ Read Matthew 27:11-26.

Like a lamb led to the slaughter, Jesus was the pure Lamb of God. He did not defend Himself. For no sin of His own was He condemned and sadly no one protested. To complete the humiliation, Jesus is led to the Praetorium, the headquarters of the Roman military.

→ Read Matthew 27:27-31.

The thorns were 3-inches long and were jammed into His head. The purple robe was draped over the open gouges from the scourging on His back, soaking up the blood. Later when it is ripped off it will reopen these wounds. He was mocked and jeered as "king of the Jews" and yet, Jesus, who could have called down legions of angels, submitted His will to that of His Father. Jesus remained silent and took it all for you and for me. He was truly a lamb led to the slaughter.

? If this week is the climax of this Grand Story, what is God hoping the readers of this story are thinking right now? What are the disciples thinking? What are you thinking?

_____

_____

_____

Day Three: Crucifixion and Burial

Crucifixion was the worst form of punishment, reserved only for criminals. It was a public display of Roman rule. In the case of Jesus, it was man's way of slamming the door shut on this man's claim to be the king of the Jews. The scene was anything but kingly, or so they thought.

➔ Read Luke 23:26-31.

❓ Why was Jesus so callous to the mourners?

These women were "professional" mourners, whose job was to follow criminals condemned to die. They were not showing true remorse. Later we will learn that only the three Marys and the disciple, John, were there with real remorse. Everyone else was there for the spectacle.

➔ Read Luke 23:32-34 and then read the two Old Testament prophesies.
➔ Read Isaiah 53:12.

❓ How is this one fulfilled?

➔ Read Psalm 22:14.

❓ How is this one fulfilled?

Jesus indeed poured out His life because it was a choice. At any point He could have said, "No." He was numbered with the transgressors, suffering a criminal's death, executed between two thieves, and He made intercession for one in particular and for all of us by proxy.

➔ Read Mark 15:23-24 and then read the three Old Testament prophecies.
➔ Read Psalm 22:14.

❓ How is this one fulfilled?

➔ Read Psalm 22:16-18.

? How is this one fulfilled?

➔ Read Psalm 69:21.

? How is this one fulfilled?

When a man was crucified, literally every bone would become disjointed by the weight of the body hanging on the cross. A jeering, gloating crowd gathered at the site, and the guards offered gall–a pain numbing drug–which He refused. No doubt Jesus' heart melted with sorrow and heartbreak. Eventually, His heart will stop but not before He suffers more.

➔ Read Mark 15:33-36 and read the Old Testament prophecy.
➔ Read Psalm 22:1.

? How is this one fulfilled?

There is no accident that Jesus quotes King David. As Christians we've come to understand this as the moment when the sins of the world are heaped upon Jesus. It is said the sins are so great that God, who is holy, is forced to turn His face, taking David's plea to another level.

➔ Read John 19:28-30 and the Old Testament prophecy fulfilled.
➔ Read Psalm 69:20.

? Why did He take the vinegar and not the gall?

He refused the gall, which included a poisonous herb such as hemlock or poppy juice, meant to dull the pain. The vinegar was a kind gesture to wet His lips just enough that He could utter His last words, "It is finished." His job was done. He obeyed even unto death. What happens next has huge spiritual implications.

➔ Read Mark 15:38-39 and the Old Testament reference.
➔ Read Hebrews 9:1-9.

? What is the significance of the curtain being torn?

The curtain was a constant reminder that sin separated people from the presence of God. Only on the Day of Atonement was the High Priest permitted to go behind the curtain to atone for the sins of the people with the blood of a lamb. Jesus became our High Priest *and* was the Holy Lamb of God, whose shed blood once and for all made sacrifice for all of our sins. His act of atonement tore the curtain, thus ending the division between God and humankind.

➔ Read John 19:31-34 and the prophecy fulfilled.
➔ Read Exodus 12:46.
? How does this apply to Jesus?

The sacrificial system instituted following the Exodus was a symbol pointing to what would be the final sacrifice–Jesus was our perfect sacrifice. He was without blemish, and His bones were never broken.

➔ Read John 19:38-42.
? Who were Joseph and Nicodemus?

Joseph was a wealthy member of the Sanhedrin who was looking for the coming of the kingdom and he became a member of that kingdom before Jesus' death. Likewise, Nicodemus was also a member of the Sanhedrin and, presumably, had come to believe that Jesus was the promised Messiah. The burial they provide is one given to a king–He was their King, and now He was dead.

➔ Read Matthew 27:62-66.

The tomb is sealed. Because of the faithfulness of these two men, God's only Son was allowed a burial, and this burial would allow you and I to hear a message—a message from within a tomb.

? What message do you hear? Are there things buried deep within your soul, keeping you from experiencing Easter morning? Do you hear the cries of the women who have seen all their hopes and dreams die before their eyes? Have you watched as unmet expectations, unfulfilled dreams, or buried hopes have hardened a large stone across the entrance to your heart? Are the wounds of life so deep there seems to be no way out of the tomb, no hope that God could forgive, no possibility of healing? Write them down and offer them to God in prayer.

The tomb is real. The death that comes with it is real, too. Jesus was laid in a tomb and the entry was sealed shut. The stench of death filled the air, it was cold and dark inside. Hope was lost.

Day Four: Resurrection

Over and over again Jesus foretold of His resurrection, but the message never got through.

Read these passages and record what was predicted.

➔ Read John 2:18-22.
➔ Read Matthew 12:39-40.
➔ Read Mark 8:31.
➔ Read Matthew 17:22.
➔ Read Luke 9:22.

In spite of these clear predictions, only the women who'd come to perform the grim task of anointing the body with oils–a task not fully done prior to burial because of the Sabbath–were at the tomb.

➔ Read John 20:1-2.

? What did Mary Magdalene assume?

_____

➔ Read Luke 24:1-8.

? What did the women assume?

_____

Their first thought was that the body had been taken. Even though they'd heard Jesus predict what would happen, they were not looking for a risen Lord. They were looking for a body. It wasn't until much later that they began to put together what Jesus' had said and what their Scriptures had predicted with what they witnessed.

➔ Read Psalm 16:10.

? Who was saying this and to whom?

_____

Although David wrote Psalm 16, it is clear to us today that this is Jesus speaking to His Father. The followers of Jesus will eventually come to understand this as Jesus–He is the faithful One whom God will not let decay. But this understanding took time. On that first Easter morning, when the women told the disciples what they'd witnessed, the disciples didn't believe the women anymore than the women believed before they had seen it with their own eyes.

➔ Read John 20:3-10.

We must admit that belief in the bodily resurrection is foolhardy to all but those who take that leap of faith. As it must have been to those present on that first resurrection day, this was too much to take in to the human mind. Sometimes we forgot how strange this belief is to the rest of the world, unless we go back to these early accounts and read them at face value. In fact, it isn't until the coming of the Holy Spirit at Pentecost, forty days later, that we get our first real understanding of what happened on the cross and in the tomb from one of those who witnessed these events.

Spend the rest of today's study time slowly reading Peter's explanation of what Jesus' death and resurrection meant. Then make your own notes.

_____

_____

_____

_____

➔ Read Acts 2:14-41.

? What was the purpose of Jesus' death? His resurrection?

_____

_____

_____

Day Five: Appearances and Ascension

Jesus will spend forty days on Earth before returning to heaven. From these accounts we learn something about Jesus, something about the disciples, and something about us. Read the Scriptures and record what you learn about each group of people.

➔ Read Luke 24:13-32.

? What did you learn about Jesus?

_____

? What did you learn about the disciples?

_____

? What did you learn about believers to come?

_____

Jesus explained that He had to suffer to fulfill the law and the prophets. In other words, Jesus was the plan from the beginning. Everything in the law and everything the prophets foretold were about Jesus. Even though they knew it was the third day, and their Messiah had prophesied about what would happen, and even though the women and a few of the disciples had seen the empty tomb, they could not make the connection. It wasn't until their eyes were opened when Jesus broke the bread, that they could see. If you "see" today, thank God for the gift because it is only when our eyes are opened by Him that anyone can see.

➔ Read Luke 24:36-43.

? What did you learn about Jesus?

_____

? What did you learn about the disciples?

_____

? What did you learn about believers to come?

_____

In this appearance and in the one before, Jesus suddenly appears and disappears and, yet, He is fully human in appearance. He speaks, He eats, and He has scars. He has a physical body and, yet, He can walk through walls and doors. He has a resurrection body. Again He reiterates that everything that happened to Him was to fulfill the Law, the Prophets, and the Psalms. The disciples still struggled to understand, but then Jesus opened their minds to the Scriptures. Again, we cannot understand, nor expect anyone else to understand, the Scriptures unless God enables that understanding.

➔ Read John 20:24-29.

? What did you learn about Jesus?

_____

? What did you learn about the disciples?

_____

? What did you learn about believers to come?

_____

Poor Thomas gets a bad rap. Instead of being called doubting Thomas he ought to be called Believing Thomas, because all of us begin from a place of doubt before we can believe. Jesus knows this, and He comes to Thomas with love and compassion. The other disciples had seen and, thus, believed, and Jesus has no doubt the same will be true with Thomas. But you and I don't get the benefit of seeing, right? Instead, we have something that they didn't have; we have God's Word and the testimony of those who were there. Jesus says to us, we will be blessed or favored when we take that leap of faith.

➔ Read John 21:1-14.

? What did you learn about the disciples?

_____

? What did you learn about believers to come?

_____

The disciples had gone back to their lives. After all, they were fisherman and fishing is what they did. So, they are out all night and it is a bust. No fish. In the wee hours of the morning a man calls to them from the shore, "Have you caught any fish?" Not recognizing Jesus, they respond, "No." The man tells them to throw the nets on the other side of the boat. Now, one would think they'd remember that Jesus had given the same instructions to them when He called them to follow Him. But they still didn't get it— they weren't getting any of this. Finally, when fish were swamping the boat, Peter recognized the miracle and knew it was Jesus. Sometimes you and I have to experience a miracle to recognize Jesus for who He really is.

? What miracle have you witnessed that helps you to believe in Jesus?

_____

This story does not end here. In fact, this scene is the set up for the real story that is to come. Continue reading...

→ Read John 21:15-25.

? What did you learn about Jesus?

_____

? What did you learn about believers to come?

_____

What a most compassionate thing for our Lord to do. No doubt Peter still carried great guilt for having denied knowing Jesus not once but three times. It is not a coincidence that Jesus asks Peter, "Do you love me," three times. Jesus knew Peter's need and He knows yours. He knows the deepest needs of every person and He longs to meet those needs.

? What are your deepest needs? Take time to seek the root of this need and then lay them before a loving and compassionate God–He is waiting to receive them and meet those needs as only He can.

_____

→ Read Matthew 28:16-20.

? What is said about doubt?

_____

This is one of the most amazing statements of faith. The disciples have spent forty days with the risen Lord, they've placed their hands in His sides, and they've witnessed Him walking through closed doors. He's opened the Scriptures to them. He's performed miracles. And yet, we are told, "Some doubted." Yes, it is a statement of faith because faith doesn't mean an absence of doubt. Faith means holding on to belief in spite of doubt. Next week we will look at the foundations of our faith explored in the writings of Paul and the other followers of Jesus. As we close this week, spend time thanking God for the events explored this week, even those things that you have difficulty fully understanding.

Small Group Study Outline

Week Four Review

Begin by reviewing the daily lessons, asking for each person's questions and the insights they gained. Ask them to summarize each day's main point.

Discussion Questions

1. How do you react to the statement that Jesus was not a New Testament plan–He was the plan all along?

2. On Day Two the author states that this week of Jesus' life is the climax of this story. What did you learn about this week, and how do these details heighten your impression of this climax?

3. On Day Three, Old Testament prophecies were set side-by-side with the New Testament story. What did you learn from this?

4. Spend a few minutes reviewing Acts 2:14-41. What does Peter's explanation of Christ's death and resurrection clear up for you?

5. On Day Five you were asked to look at a series of verses and detail what you learned about Jesus, the disciples, and future believers. What did you learn overall about each?

6. The author calls the fact that "some doubted" an amazing statement of faith. Do you agree? How does this change the way you see your own doubts?

WEEK FIVE
NEW COVENANT: THE MISSION CONTINUES

Day One: Through Your Seed

One of the things the Jews struggled to come to terms with was the teachings that seemed to counter what they'd been taught about faith. Was this a new faith? If it was a continuation of what the Scriptures taught, how were they to view the faith of Abraham that had been handed down to them through generations? What were they to do with the idea that now the Gentiles are included? Paul, a good and faithful Jew, sought to answer this question in his letter to the Roman church.

➔ Read Romans 3:9-17.

❓ Who is Paul quoting?

_____

By quoting the great prophet Isaiah, Paul is pointing out that this has been God's message from the beginning. No one–not a Gentile or a Jew–has measured up. Just because the Jews were chosen doesn't make them sinless. So how were the Jews, or the Gentiles for that matter, ever going to be who God made them to be–sinless? Again Paul answers.

➔ Read Romans 3:21-26.

❓ How are we to be justified, or righted, to God?

_____

_____

Paul explains that all we've witnessed throughout Scripture was a demonstration of God's forbearance, His grace. Sins of both the Gentiles and the Jews deserved punishment, but God allowed all those sins to go unpunished so He could demonstrate that only He was just and could justify. God, through Jesus, justifies us through faith in Jesus. As confusing as this might sound to us today, you can imagine how it must have sounded to the newly believing Jews with whom Paul was speaking. So Paul gives an example that every Jew would understand.

➔ Read Romans 4:1-12.

❓ How is Abraham the Father of both the Jews and the Gentiles?

_____

Abraham believed God, and through that faith he was called righteous, not because he was perfect or good or did good things, but because he believed. Then he was circumcised as an outward sign of a heart pierced by God. The Jews had come to see circumcision as a sign of their choseness, which was partially true. They were chosen as set apart–pure and holy. Paul is setting the record straight. Abraham was circumcised *after* he believed and was called righteous. Righteousness comes by faith alone. But what about all of those Old Testament laws? Paul answers that question, too.

➔ Read Romans 4:13-16.

❓ What is the connection between the law and faith?

Paul puts it plainly–if you only have the law and can follow all of them, then faith is made worthless. He says the law only brings wrath. In other words, the whole point of the law was to show us how far we'd fallen from perfection. It was to show us how much we needed a Savior.

Again Paul addresses faith in his letter to the Hebrews. Chapter eleven is often called the faith chapter. It is long so we will end today's lesson so you have time to read this important chapter. As you read, count how many faithful people Paul references by name.

➔ Read Hebrews 11.

❓ How many faithful people are referenced?

From the beginning of this chapter Paul defines faith as having hope. Sometimes we confuse faith with confidence and having no doubt, but the certainty comes in believing in something we cannot see and to which we hold fast even as we doubt. These fifteen people and the faithful who followed them had doubts, still sinned, and yet held fast to their hope in a God who was faithful to fulfill His promises.

We end this day by reading a familiar verse, which is often divorced from the chapter that you just read. As you read this hopeful promise, notice that it begins with the word, 'therefore.'

➔ Read Hebrews 12:1-3.

❓ How does the preceding chapter change how you read this verse? How does today's readings change the way you view hope and faith?

Day Two: A Blessing

God's promise to Abraham was that he would be a blessing and through his offspring that blessing would continue. Although God was clear, the message became muddled through the generations and the purpose of being blessed was turned inward. So the first act of the Holy Spirit following Jesus' ascension was to demonstrate in a tangible way the purpose of blessing.

➔ Read Acts 2:1-12.

? How and to whom did the believers become a blessing?

_____

What follows next is Peter's address to the crowd and in verse 41 we see that more than three-thousand speaking fifteen different languages heard the message of salvation through Yeshua in their native language, and they believed. But the blessings did not stop there.

➔ Read Acts 2:42-47.

? How were they further blessed and how did they continue the blessings?

_____

_____

They were blessed with the gifts and talents they needed, and the people used those gifts to serve each other. They performed wondrous signs and miracles as their awe increased, and as they pooled their resources they realized they had more than enough to share with others. Furthermore, as they worshipped their joy increased and they were given favor in the community. Finally, God added to their numbers so their blessings could continue to spread.

However, after a short time the blessing took a form that confuses us even today. Persecution swept through the Christian community and caused them to flee. It might not have appeared to be a blessing at the time, but today we know the Christian faith never would have expanded if this time of persecution had not come. Because of persecution, believers dispersed, including Peter who went to Joppa. At the same time, in the nearby town of Caesarea, a Gentile man named Cornelius had a visit from an angel who told him to send for Peter and to listen to what Peter had to say. In the meantime, Peter also had a vision. He saw a sheet lowered from heaven by four corners. On it were all kinds of unclean animals and a voice told Peter to kill and eat. Peter refused, but the voice told him not to call anything impure that God made clean. After the vision, men sent by Cornelius arrived to invite Peter to come. Peter went. After hearing from Cornelius, Peter connected his vision with the Gentiles before him. Read Peter's explanation of what happened.

➔ Read Acts 11:4-18.

? What was undeniable to Peter and the other apostles?

_____

Peter asks, after explaining how Cornelius' whole family were baptized in the Holy Spirit, "Who was I to think I could oppose God."

? What is God doing around you that you are struggling to accept?

God blesses whom He chooses to bless and sometimes it is difficult to understand what He is doing. Sometimes we struggle because it is counter to all that we feel is right, just, and fair. Peter had been a good and faithful Jew, and now 'these people' who did not follow all the rules he'd been faithful in were receiving the same blessings. What Peter didn't know was how faithful Cornelius had been. Peter didn't know Cornelius' heart, but God did. Cornelius and all others like him (you and me) were God's goal in blessing Abraham and his descendants.

Now the apostles were convinced, but the believing Jews still struggled. As the numbers of Gentile believers increased the issue became a problem that needed to be addressed. And who better to address this issue than Saul, who became Paul. Read his response.

➜ Read Romans 11:1-6.

Did you read that? God has been a God of grace all along. Every time His people failed, God extended grace. Yes, there was wrath and that wrath was always deserved, but the grace was undeserved.

➜ Read Romans 11:13-15.
? How does envy play a part in blessing?

Envy is not a godly attribute, but God sometimes uses envy to show us what we are missing. Paul explains that many of his fellows Jews did not believe, but perhaps through their envy in seeing God's blessings on the Gentiles they might be drawn to the faith.

? What is envy showing you right now?

➜ Read Romans 11:17-18.
? Who is the Olive Shoot? Who are the cut off branches and who are the grafted in branches?

Jesus is the shoot from the stump of Jesse (Isaiah 11:1), non-believing Jews are the cut-off branches, and believing Gentiles are those that are grafted in. In Israel today, the grafted-in symbol, which combines the menorah, the Star of David, and the Christian fish, signify a Gentile who recognizes the grace that has been extended to them through Jesus the Christ.

➔ Read Romans 11:19-22.

? What do these verses warn against and what do they encourage us to do?

We are warned against arrogance because faith is only enabled by grace, and we are encouraged to extend the kindness that has been given to us by God to all those around us. We are blessed so we can be a blessing.

Day Three: All Pointing to Jesus

You may have heard that because humankind could not follow the rules God set forth, God sent Jesus. This is somewhat misleading. Yes, we could not follow the rules and, yes, Jesus was the answer. But Jesus was the answer all along. God didn't try something and discover it didn't work so Jesus was his Plan B. As we will read today, Jesus was God's answer from Adam forward.

➔ Read Romans 5:12-19.

❓ What is Adam called?

Adam was a pattern or template because his selfishness led to sin just as our selfishness leads us to sin. Here Paul makes it clear that the law is not what brings death (if you remember in our Old Testament study, the law came later)–it is sin that brings death to our souls. The same sin that led to Adam and Eve's banishment from the place of peace and harmony called the Garden of Eden–their desire to be their own gods–is the same sin that leads us astray today. We want our own way. We want to make our own decisions and do things that are contrary to Scripture. In this way, Adam is a pattern for us, but the good news is that Adam was also a pattern for Christ.

❓ How is Adam like Jesus?

Verse 17 says it well: through one man (and woman) sin/death reigned, and through one man, Jesus Christ, grace/life reigned. Verses 19 adds that through Adam's disobedience all were made sinners, but through the obedience of Jesus all who trust and believe were made righteous.

➔ Read Colossians 1:15-23.

❓ What is Jesus called?

Paul wants us to know that Jesus was there from the creation of the world. He wasn't Plan B. He is God with skin on–the exact representation of God. Jesus is the firstborn of all creation. He was not simply a prophet or a good teacher. Paul deftly explains that only Jesus, as both divine and human, could be the means to humankind's salvation. Jesus was created before the world for this purpose, because God knew we would need a Savior.

➔ Read Colossians 2:9-15.

❓ How is the practice of circumcision a picture of Christ?

Circumcision, as prescribed in Genesis 17:9-14, was always to point to our commitment to God–a pierced heart. It was to be an outward sign of an inward piercing–a contrite spirit before a holy God.

? What Christian practice is circumcision related to?

_____

Like circumcision was the sign of the covenant, baptism is the sign of the new covenant. Jeremiah predicted the coming of a new covenant nearly six-hundred-years before Christ's death and resurrection.

→ Read Jeremiah 31:31-33.

? What stays the same in the new covenant and what is different?

_____

God desires to be the one and only God and for His people to pledge their loyalty to only Him–I will be their God and they will be My people. This has not changed. However, the old covenant was written on stone tablets and the new covenant is written on our hearts.

→ Read Luke 22:20.

? How is the cup the symbol of the new covenant?

_____

When Jesus took the cup, He said this was the cup of the new covenant–His blood poured out for you and for me.

→ Read Hebrews 9:1-10 to remind yourself of the first covenant's rules for the priest and for making sacrifices. What was the role of the blood sacrifice made by the High Priest once a year on the Day of Atonement?

→ Read Hebrews 9:11-15 to understand how Jesus became our High Priest, using His own blood to redeem us once and for all, setting us free from slavery to sin and death. Jesus was the unblemished Lamb, whose blood cleanses our consciences from the guilt of sin.

? Are you struggling with guilt from past sins? Make a list.

_____

If you've asked for forgiveness from God, know that your sins are gone–washed away by the blood of the Lamb. Remembering those same sins is often a ploy of Satan, who does not want you to experience the freedom Jesus has already paid for you to receive. The next time that memory returns, ask God if there is anything there for you to still repent of, and if He tells you that you are free–then tell Satan to get behind you. You are accepting the freedom Christ is offering.

→ Read Hebrews 10:1-17 and record what God says remembering your sins and lawless acts.

As far as the east is from the west, your sins are flung. Don't be surprised when you go to God with memories of past sins you've already brought before Him that God says, "I have no idea what you are talking about for that sin has been forgiven and forgotten." We often hear that to forgive is to forget, but that statement is misleading. Only God truly forgets. Remembering our sins is a human trait that causes us to seek forgiveness and release from the prison of condemnation. Yet, continuing to seek forgiveness for sins that have been forgiven is to deny the gift of the blood sacrifice of our perfect Lamb and our High Priest. So, don't fall into that trap, which is a ploy of Satan to keep you from living in God's freedom.

Day Four: To All Nations

The covenant with Abraham declared that he and his seed were to be a blessing to all nations. The "all nations" part of this promise would be fulfilled most boldly in the missionary journeys of Paul.

➔ Read Acts 13:42-52.

? Who rejected the gospel and who received it?

_____

The Jews in Antioch were happy to hear Paul speak to them about being God's chosen people and about Abraham's covenant, but when Paul explained how the gospel fulfilled this covenant, the Jews rejected him and his message. On the other hand, the Gentiles who heard the same message openly received the good news.

? In verse 47, what chapter and verse from the Old Testament was Paul quoting?

_____

Isaiah 49:6 was a prophecy fulfilled in the life of Jesus, and it was continued in the missionary work of Paul. It still continues today as we share the good news with all people in every nation.

The fact that Gentiles were coming to faith in Christ at such a rapid pace began to cause conflict.

➔ Read Acts 15:1-5 and describe what the central issue was.

The Jewish apostles and followers of this new way were insisting on the adherence to Jewish laws including the one on circumcision. Paul was converting thousands upon thousands of Gentiles who did not have the same ties to Jewish law. So they convened what would be the first church council. Read Peter's address to the council.

➔ Read Acts 15:6-11.

? Summarize Paul's argument.

_____

_____

Paul said, "Look at what God is doing. Who are we to declare unclean what God is making clean?" He said, "It is all about grace and it has been from the beginning." When Paul finished, James addressed the assembly.

➔ Read Acts 15:13-21.

? What did James argue?

James, the brother of Jesus who would become the leader of the Jerusalem church, begins by quoting from the prophet Amos who clearly states that God's message will include the Gentiles. He then says this new way should not be made difficult for new converts and, yet, the laws of Moses are not to be abandoned. Then they crafted a letter to explain their understanding.

→ Read Acts 15:24-29.

? What were the main requirements from the law?

Christians were to abstain from foods sacrificed to idols, from blood, from the meat of strangled animals, and from sexual immorality. Later Paul clarified the purpose of these rules.

→ Read 1 Corinthians 8:4-13.

? Why did Paul say the food restrictions were maintained?

The church in Syrian Antioch, comprised of both Jews and Gentiles, struggled with this issue. This decision was made not to promote legalism but to keep peace within the church. So, when they gathered as a church family to eat, those who desired to adhere to the Jewish laws would know they could eat freely and those to whom the issue was really a non-issue would not cause their brother or sister in the faith to go against his or her conscience. This was a decision to deny oneself for the sake of another.

The food laws were not the only obstacles for Jews and Gentiles coming to the faith. There was still much confusion over how all that they had been taught and had sought to follow in Jewish law now worked in this new faith. Read Paul's answer to the church at Galatia.

→ Read Galatians 3:7-9.

? Who would be blessed?

All nations would be blessed if they relied on faith. Next, Paul contrasts faith to those who rely on their ability to follow the law.

→ Read Galatians 3:10-14.

? What did the law do? What did Jesus do?

The law demonstrated for us the curse that our sin had placed us under. It was a visible way for God to show us the depth of our inability to follow even the simplest of laws. Sin is so deceptive, and so without the law we were condemned to blindness. The good news is that the law was meant to help us see our need for a Savior, for not even the best human being in the world could "be holy," as we were required to be.

? What laws are you struggling to follow today?

Following the written and unwritten rules of Christianity is a fulltime job for a lot of Christians. For them the concept of grace seems simply too good to be true. Our consciences condemn us. Satan condemns us. The law condemns us. Our sins condemn us. Yet, God in his limitless grace sets us free from all condemnation. *This* is the new covenant under which we live–the covenant of grace. It is *new,* not because grace wasn't here before Jesus, but only because Jesus had to justify us to or make us right with God, who is and was always grace. Read how Paul explains this.

→ Read Galatians 3:15-25.

So the law was our guardian until Christ came, and now we live under the law of grace, if we choose to trust in that grace.

If you still struggle with law and grace, ask God to help you cut those chains and receive the freedom you were meant to receive in grace.

Day Five: The Apostles' Creed

Perhaps the best known creedal or faith statement is what is today called the Apostles' Creed. The original germ of it is thought to be the confession made by converts to Christianity at their baptism. The earliest form was found in the Old Roman Form and dates to the middle of the 2nd century (about 140 AD).

Today we will examine both the Old and New Testament scriptures, which are believed to have formed this confession of faith. Make a note for yourself as you look up each reference.

I believe in God, the Father Almighty,
> ➜ Read Isaiah 44:6.
> ➜ Read John 1:1-3.

Maker of heaven and earth.
> ➜ Read Genesis 1:1.
> ➜ Read Acts 14:15.

And in Jesus Christ,
> ➜ Read Deuteronomy 18:18-18.
> ➜ Read Luke 2:11.

His only Son,
> ➜ Read Proverbs 30:4.
> ➜ Read John 3:16.

our Lord,
> ➜ Read Isaiah 45:5.
> ➜ Read John 20:28.

who was conceived by the Holy Spirit,
> ➜ Read Jeremiah 31:22.
> ➜ Read Luke 1:35.

born of the Virgin Mary,
> ➜ Read Isaiah 7:14.
> ➜ Read Luke 1:26-27.

suffered under Pontius Pilate,
> ➜ Read Zechariah 12:10.
> ➜ Read Luke 23:23-25.

was crucified,
> ➜ Read Psalm 22.
> ➜ Read John 19:20.

dead
- ➔ Read Psalm 16.
- ➔ Read 1 Corinthians 15:3.

and buried.
- ➔ Read Isaiah 53:9.
- ➔ Read 1 Corinthians 15:4.

He descended into Hell.
- ➔ Read Zechariah 12:10.
- ➔ Read 1 Peter 3:18b-20a.

The third day He arose from the dead.
- ➔ Read Hosea 6:2.
- ➔ Read Acts 4:10.

He ascended into Heaven,
- ➔ Read Psalm 68:18.
- ➔ Read Luke 24:51.

and is seated at the right hand of God,
- ➔ Read Psalm 110:1.
- ➔ Read Hebrews 1:3.

the Father Almighty.
- ➔ Read Deuteronomy 6:4.
- ➔ Read Galatians 3:26.

From thence He shall come to judge the quick and the dead.
- ➔ Read Isaiah 49:2.
- ➔ Read 2 Timothy 4:1.

I believe in the Holy Spirit,
- ➔ Read Joel 2:28-29.
- ➔ Read John 15:26.

the church universal (or Holy catholic church),
- ➔ Read Jeremiah 32:39.
- ➔ Read John 17:21.

the communion of saints,
- ➔ Read Psalm 133:1.
- ➔ Read Hebrews 21.1.

the forgiveness of sins,
- ➔ Read Isaiah 53:10.
- ➔ Read Luke 7:48.

the resurrection of the body,
- ➔ Read Job 19:25-26.
- ➔ Read 1 Thessalonians 4:16.

and life everlasting.
- ➔ Read 2 Samuel 7.
- ➔ Read John 10:28.

? How has this exercise changed the way you hear the Apostles' Creed? What new insights have you gained?

_____

_____

_____

The Apostles' Creed seems to represent some form of what the early church called the "rule of faith" or core teachings. Signs of these "core teachings" are seen as early as the New Testament book of Hebrews. The Apostles' Creed represents a set of uncompromisable core beliefs for Christians. It beautifully ties together truths from both the Old Testament and the New. Next week we will look at the truths found in both the Old and New Testaments detailing how we are to live as God's People.

Small Group Study Outline

Week Five Review

Begin by reviewing the daily lessons, asking for each person's questions and the insights they gained. Ask them to summarize each day's main point.

Discussion Questions

1. This week was titled, The Mission Continues. How did the study of the Old Testament in light of the New, show you that the mission was and always has been the same?

2. How does faith and law intersect? How does doubt play with faith?

3. How were the people of God to be a blessing? What did God do to demonstrate His definition?

4. Have you heard the argument that because humankind could not follow the law, God decided to send Jesus? How has this study changed or tweaked your understanding of this statement?

5. How did you react to the author's statement that when you bring to God a sin for which He's already forgiven you, don't be surprised when He says, "What sin?"

6. Do you agree that without the law we were condemned to blindness? How does sin make us blind?

7. On Day Five you looked at the Apostles' Creed and the Old Testament underpinnings for this Christian statement of faith. How did this exercise change the way you hear the Apostles' Creed?

WEEK SIX
THE WAY: LIVING AS GOD'S PEOPLE

Day One: Commandments

Almost sixty years after His death and resurrection, Jesus revealed what the culmination of His story would look like. In the Book of Revelation, Jesus, through the author John, makes two bold statements about the commandments of God.

In the Book of Revelation, God identifies faithful members of His Church as those "who keep the commandments" (Revelation 12:17). In fact, the final words of the Bible and of this revelation likewise state: "Blessed are those who do His commandments, that they may have the right to the tree of life, and may enter through the gates into the city" (Revelation 22:14).

➔ Read Revelations 12:17.

? Who are the faithful members of God's church?

_____

Those who keep the commandments of God are called faithful.

➔ Read Revelations 22:14.

? Who are the blessed that may enter into the gates of heaven?

_____

Blessed are those who do what the Lord God commands. When early believers heard the word *commandments*, they would have first thought of the Ten Commandments given by Moses to the People of God. It was important for God's people, both the Jews and Gentiles, to know that the Ten Commandments were not just an old covenant thing. They applied to the lives of the followers of Yeshua just as they did to the followers of Yahweh.

Today we will examine both the Old Testament and the New Testament Scriptural support for the Ten Commandments. When you look up each reference, make note of what the commandment is in the Old Testament and what new insight you gain from the New.

The First Commandment
    ➔ Read Deuteronomy 5:7.
    ➔ Read Matthew 4:10.

The Second Commandment
    ➔ Read Deuteronomy 5:8-10.
    ➔ Read Acts 15:20.

The Third Commandment
    ➔ Read Deuteronomy 5:11.
    ➔ Read James 2:7.

The Fourth Commandment
➜ Read Deuteronomy 5:12-15.
➜ Read 1 John 2:6.

The Fifth Commandment
➜ Read Deuteronomy 5:16.
➜ Read Luke 18:20.

The Sixth Commandment
➜ Read Deuteronomy 5:17.
➜ Read Mark 10:19.

The Seventh Commandment
➜ Read Deuteronomy 5:18.
➜ Read Luke 16:18.

The Eighth Commandment
➜ Read Deuteronomy 5:19.
➜ Read Matthew 19:18.

The Ninth Commandment
➜ Read Deuteronomy 5:20.
➜ Read Ephesians 4:25.

The Tenth Commandment
➜ Read Deuteronomy 5:21.
➜ Read Romans 1:29.

? How has this exercise changed how you view the Ten Commandments?

? Why do you think John included his words about following the commandments in his Book of Revelation?

The Ten Commandments were not just rules for us to follow, they were a sort of resume' of who God is and how we are to relate to Him and to each other if we call ourselves children of God. In other words, this is part of our DNA as members of God's family.

Which one of the Ten Commandments do you find the easiest to follow and which one(s) do you find the most difficult? Ask God to help you follow His commandments, not because you want to follow the rules, but because you want to represent Him well in this world.

Day Two: The Beatitudes and Two Greats

Many call the Beatitudes 'the New Testament's Ten Commandments.' The word Beatitude comes from the Latin word meaning blessed or happy and, thus, in sharing these Beatitudes Jesus is sharing the way Christians can lead a happy or blessed life. Each Beatitude consists of two phrases–the condition and the result. The condition is an Old Testament reference, and the result is the new interpretation Jesus places on it.

As we did yesterday, we will look up both the Old Testament 'condition' and the new interpretation of it in the Book of Matthew. Fill in the blanks for each and then look up the Old Testament reference, making note of what you learn.

Matthew 5:3.
Blessed are the _____; for _____.
Psalm 37:11.

Matthew 5:4.
Blessed are the _____; for _____.
Isaiah 61:2.

Matthew 5:5.
Blessed are the _____; for _____.
Psalm 25:9.

Matthew 5:6.
Blessed are the _____; for _____.
Isaiah 25:6

Matthew 5:7.
Blessed are the _____; for _____.
Micah 7:18.

Matthew 5:8.
Blessed are the _____; for _____.
Psalm 24:4.

Matthew 5:9.
Blessed are the _____; for _____.
Proverbs 12:20.

Matthew 5:10.
Blessed are the _____; for _____.
Isaiah 51:7.

Two other commandments in the New Testament deserve inspection. The first is often called the Great Commission.

➔ Read Matthew 28:19.

❓ What does it mean to "go and make disciples?"

The word "go" is an active verb and it means to continuously go out, to not stay in one place. In other words, we are to leave the safety and security of our homes and churches and share Jesus. This can take many forms, but it is clear Christianity would never have grown beyond the twelve had the disciples not taken risks–had they not 'gone.'

❓ Where are you 'going' beyond your comfort zone? Ask God to show you who needs to hear about Jesus in your corner of the world.

Jesus calls the last commandment we will examine today the Greatest Commandment and it follows what Jesus calls the most important one.

➔ Read Mark 12:28-34.

❓ What is the first commandment to which Jesus refers?

Jesus quotes the prayer taken from Deuteronomy 6:4 called the Shema, which was spoken daily in Jewish worship because it sums up all ten of the commandments. However, Jesus didn't leave it there. He added that we are also to love our neighbor as ourselves. He then tells us there is no greater commandment than these.

If we read all of them together, we not only get a picture of what it means to live a Christian life, we also know what it means to live as Christ–the perfect image of God.

❓ What do you find the most difficult of these teachings?

❓ What one thing do you plan to do this week to help you reflect these Christ-like qualities more fully?

The Ten Commandments, the Great Commission or Commandment, and the Greatest Commandment are a part of God's Grand story and His message to us about how we are to live as God's People–holy as He is holy.

Day Three: Duty

As members of God's kingdom, we've sworn allegiance to a new way of living—Kingdom Living. Said another way, we have a duty to live out our lives in accordance with Kingdom rules. These rules are counter to the way others live or the way in which our world operates. As we read through these passages, make a note of what is called for and also what the opposite of living this way would mean.

➔ Read Romans 12:1-2.

? How are we called to live?

_____

? What would be the opposite?

_____

We are called to live as holy sacrifices before the altar of God, which means we must purify and cleanse ourselves in mind and word and deed. The opposite would be to continue as corrupted and sinful beings, never examining our thoughts, words, and actions.

➔ Read Romans 12:3.

? How are we called to live?

_____

? What would be the opposite?

_____

We are called to live humbly. The opposite would be to live proud, haughty, and puffed up.

➔ Read Romans 12:9-16.

? How are we called to live?

_____

? What would be the opposite?

_____

These eight verses summarize what it means to live in love with the doors of our hearts and lives open wide. To live the opposite is to be stingy, closed off, fearful, and selfish.

➔ Read Ephesians 4:20-28.
? How are we called to live?

_____

? What would be the opposite?

_____

We are to speak truth, rein in our anger, and not only pay our own way but earn enough to bless others. To live the opposite is to do whatever feels good, whether it harms another or not. To live the opposite is to live life allowing our emotions to rule, and to take regardless if it has been earned or not.

➔ Read Ephesians 4:29-32.
? How are we called to live?

_____

? What would be the opposite?

_____

We are to use our words to bless and we're to be kind, compassionate, and forgiving. We are also called to get rid of all bitterness, rage and anger, brawling and slander, and every form of evil intention. To live the opposite is to allow our words to wound and destroy, and to allow anger to fuel our days, leading us to dismiss evil intentions as justified.

➔ Read Ephesians 5:3-5.
? How are we called to live?

_____

? What would be the opposite?

_____

We are called to live pure and consecrated lives having no other god before our God including sexual desires, greed, obscene language or viewing anything that would be obscene. To live the opposite is to make sex or sexuality our god, to make the accumulation of wealth our god, or the things we wish to say or view our gods.

➔ Read 1 John 3:4-6.
? How are we called to live?

_____

? What would be the opposite?

_____

We are to live free of the need to sin–not that we won't ever sin–but we are to live as ones not held captive by our sins. To live the opposite is to believe we are helpless to stop sinning.

➔ Read 2 Corinthians 9:6-8.

? How are we called to live?

_____

? What would be the opposite?

_____

We are to live generously, giving with joy, knowing that all good things comes from God and meant to be shared. To live the opposite is to live stingy, believing we've earned everything and there is little to go around so we must hold fast to what we have.

➔ Read Ephesians 4:3-6.

? How are we called to live?

_____

? What would be the opposite?

_____

We are to live as one body, united in harmony and peace. To live the opposite is to live at odds with one another as if we are at war, seeing one another as competition or, worse, as enemies.

This is our duty, our calling, our pledge of allegiance. Kingdom living requires dying to our selfish ways and living for others, with others, and because of others. It is living in opposition to a world that tells us to live for ourselves. It is the way Jesus lived, and died–for others.

Day Four: Problems

Many would sign-on to this kingdom way of living, even knowing the duties examined yesterday, if it weren't for the promised problems we are told are coming. Christians are warned that with faith in Christ comes suffering–it's guaranteed.

→ Read 1 Peter 4:12-16.

? How do you think God's glory is revealed in your suffering?

_____

→ Read James 1:2-4.

Suffering is meant to test or strengthen our faith, producing steadfastness. After time, continued steadfastness will produce a strong character, complete in every way and perfectly reflecting Christ. This is how we demonstrate God's glory.

? So what kind of suffering are we talking about? Read the following passages and make notes.

→ Read 1 Peter 6-7.

_____

→ Read 1 Peter 3:13-17.

_____

→ Read 1 Peter 4:1-4.

_____

The Bible warns we should expect grief of all kinds, threats, and slander simply for doing good, and bodily harm for refusing to join in sinful behavior because in refusing it shines a spotlight on other's sin.

? So what are we to do when promised problems knock on our doors?

_____

→ Read Romans 5:3-5 and fill in the blanks.

Suffering produces _____, endurance produces _____, and character produces _____, and hope does not _____.

Some misunderstand this teaching to mean we are supposed to be grateful for cancer, for murder, for adultery, and loss. This would be mean-spirited–this is not what God is asking of us. God wants us to see the good that God can bring from our sufferings. We can rejoice 'while in the midst of' our suffering, not 'for our sufferings.' We are promised that God will help us to endure, and that endurance will build our character, and with a godly character we will hold fast to the hope our faith in Christ brings. So what is this hope?

➔ Read Romans 8:18-25.

❓ What is hope and what are we waiting for?

Hope is believing in what we can't see. What can't we see? We have yet to see evil fully defeated. We have yet to see Christ seated on His throne. We have yet to see the full rewards of our faithfulness. We have yet to see all suffering ceased. This is what we hope for–it is what we expectantly wait for, believing in what we cannot see.

➔ Read Hebrews 6:19.

❓ What is "the hope that enters behind the curtain?"

➔ Read Psalm 71:5.

Did you hear that? Hope is a person and His name is Jesus. Jesus enters into the inner place behind the curtain. As our High Priest He enters that holy place. Jesus is the sure and steadfast anchor for our soul– He is our hope and the reason we can believe in what we cannot see. Jesus is the reason we can rejoice, even while suffering, because in Him our hope of a future without suffering is made real.

As we close today's reading, slowly review this summary offered by Paul of what Jesus, our High Priest, offers us.

➔ Read Hebrews 10:19-23.

❓ What does this tell you about the hope you have in Christ?

The story is almost complete. However, one final chapter is yet to be written. Unlike any other book ever written, the Holy Bible is compiled of writings that cover a span of about 1400 years and include some 40 writers. The time period recorded during those 1400 years covers nearly 4000 years of human history and God's revelation of Himself to and through humankind. And yet, the story is not complete.

So why didn't God wrap up His story at the end of His book? The answer is that God in His great mercy is giving us time to join Him in His mission of reconciliation.

➔ Read 2 Peter 3:9.

God desires that no one parish. However, in the end judgment will come, and so will glorious joy. Tomorrow we will hear how all of this will happen. Today, spend time thanking God for being patient.

Day Five: Promises

The story is not completed. As we've already discovered, when Jesus died and rose again He ushered in the Kingdom of God. It is already here, but it is not yet fully realized. Like a newborn baby, all of that child's personality and contributions to this world are there within that tiny human body, but the promise that child has will not be fully realized until the little baby grows into maturity. The promise is not mature until the final chapter is written. The Bible gives us a hint of what the culmination of this story will look like. As Christians we believe in and trust the Lord of the future, and we lean into that future, which God has promised. So what exactly is promised?

➜ Read 1 Corinthians 15:22-26.

❓ What will happen in the end?

Christ will hand the Kingdom he inaugurated with his own life and death over to God, the Father. He will do this after He has destroyed all evil, and death is finally destroyed. So, in the end no one will ever die an earthly death again and evil will be no more.

➜ Read 1 Corinthians 15:50-54.

❓ What is this promise?

In the end we will receive new bodies that will not perish. Those who have died, and those still living, will "in a flash" receive a resurrection body. We know that Jesus was resurrected and recognized by the disciples, that His body was similar to His earthly one but it did not have the limitations of His earthly form. We don't know much about these heavenly bodies, but what we do know tells us they will be glorious.

➜ Read 2 Corinthians 5:1-7.

❓ What is the Holy Spirit's role in this promise?

The Holy Spirit is a deposit, and when Christ returns for us that deposit will be cashed in, if you will. Until then our earthly bodies will groan and creek, and cry out for what is to come. For to be in this body is to be apart from God, but once we are fully clothed in our new bodies, we will live with God in perfect communion.

➜ Read 1 Thessalonians 4:16-17.

❓ How will this happen?

We don't know all of the details, but we know it will involve trumpets, angels, and the rising of the dead. We will also be raised together with Christ in the clouds. What a glorious sight that will be.

➔ Read 2 Thessalonians 1:5-10.

? What will happen to those who do not obey God?

This promise helps us to endure the hardships we face today. Our just God will punish those who've rejected His ways, who've caused us pain, and who refuse to repent. They will suffer everlasting destruction.

The Book of Revelation is both a book about the fall of Jerusalem in 70AD, and the end of the current age and the ushering in of the promised and fulfilled Kingdom of God. Where that line is drawn is debated, but the following visions as relayed by the disciple John are clearly a picture of the conclusion of the Story of God. As you read these visions, picture yourself in the crowd of believers, clothed in your new body, and witnessing the fulfillment of the promises made to Abraham, Isaac, and Jacob. Promises made by God that we would one day be His people and He would be our One and Only True God. The promise made by Isaiah and repeated by Paul with clarity, that one day every knee would bow and every tongue would confess the name of Jesus and Lord, will be fulfilled. And the promise made by Jesus that He was going to prepare a place, and would one day return for us, will also come to pass. Read the following passages from the Book of Revelation and revel in the glory of this promised end to the Story.

➔ Read Revelation 4:1-11.

? In your own words describe this scene.

➔ Read Revelation 5:1-14.

? Who is the Lion of the tribe of Judah, the Root of David, the Lamb who opened the scroll?

Jesus is the only one who can open the Scroll.

➔ Read Revelation 7:9-17.

? Who are those in white robes?

Believers are those in white robes–you and me. Don't get caught up in the discussions of the tribulation. If we do, we lose sight of the most important parts of this vision–the promises of God being fulfilled.

➔ Read Revelation 20:12-15.

❓ Who are judged?

_____

Every person will stand before the judgment seat. If our names are in the Book of Life, we will be judged as someone washed in the blood of Christ–pure and clean. But those whose names are not in that book, they will be forever lost to death–their sin will condemn them. Note that we are not told how this will be known, and many point to the fact that at the last moment the thief on the cross was promised eternal life. What is known here is that all will be judged and some will enter eternal damnation.

➔ Read Revelation 21:1-8.

❓ What does it mean that all things will be made new?

_____

All of creation will be returned to the Shalom for which it was created. All created things will once again live in perfect harmony and unity with God the Father, Jesus the Son, and the Holy Spirit for which it was designed in the beginning. This has been God's goal, His mission, from Genesis onward.

➔ Read Revelation 22:1-5.

❓ What stands out for you in this final vision?

_____

_____

➔ Read Revelation 22:16-17.

❓ Who are invited to "Come?"

_____

The thirsty, those who can hear, and all those who accept the gift are invited to come. You don't have to be good, innocent, holy, super spiritual, or morally upright. God invites us to join Him in this mission to invite all people to "Come."

Are you thirsty? Can you hear God's small whisper in your soul? Are you willing to stretch out your hand to receive the gift of salvation being offered to you today? Then, come.

This Story is for *you*.

The mission has been from the beginning to redeem *you*.

God wrote this Story for *you*.

So, *Come*!

Small Group Study Outline

Week Six Review

Begin by reviewing the daily lessons, asking for each person's questions and the insights they gained. Ask them to summarize each day's main point.

Discussion Questions

1. On Day One we looked at both the Old and new Testament support for the Ten Commandments. What did you learn from this exercise?

2. On Day Two we looked at the conditions and the result for the Beatitudes. What did you learn?

3. On Day Three you looked up several teachings on the duty to live as Kingdom People. In reviewing the overall list, how would you define how we are to live and what the opposite be?

4. How do you see the intersection of suffering and hope?

5. On Day Four the author states that the Bible covers nearly 4000 years of history, was written over 1400 years, from 40 different authors. How does this information inform how you view the Bible and how you hear the critics of the Bible?

6. Day Five was a review of what God has promised for the end of this story. What does it mean to you that God is waiting to write this final chapter?

7. What hope do you find in the visions of what this end will look like? What promises are most meaningful to you?

8. How has this study changed the way you see the Bible as One Story? About One Mission? About One God?

If you enjoyed this study, you may enjoy Cheri's other Bible study in the Following God series, Parables and Word Pictures. In it you'll gain fresh insight from Cheri's tour of the Holy Land where the parables were first shared. It is a study that will change the way you hear the parables and the 'word pictures' Jesus used in the New Testament.

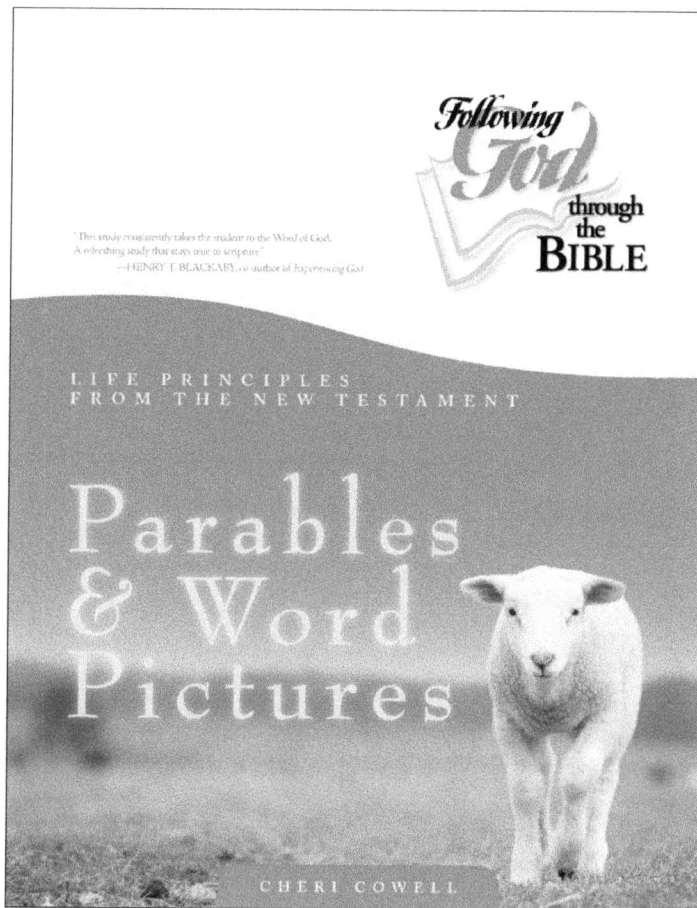

www.ingramcontent.com/pod-product-compliance
Lightning Source LLC
Chambersburg PA
CBHW081634040426
42449CB00014B/3309